EatingWell™ ON A Budget

140
DELICIOUS,
HEALTHY,
AFFORDABLE
RECIPES

AMAZING MEALS FOR LESS THAN $3 A SERVING

BY JESSIE PRICE & THE EATINGWELL TEST KITCHEN

Join us at **WWW.EATINGWELL.COM** for more delicious recipes and the inspiration and information you need to make healthy eating a way of life.

© Copyright 2010 by Eating Well, Inc., publisher of EatingWell®,
Where Good Taste Meets Good Health
823A Ferry Road, P.O. Box 1010, Charlotte, VT 05445
www.eatingwell.com

Library of Congress Cataloging-in-Publication Data has been applied for.

ISBN 978-0-88150-913-7

Published by
The Countryman Press
P.O. Box 748, Woodstock, VT 05091
Distributed by
W.W. Norton & Company, Inc.
500 Fifth Avenue, New York, NY 10110
Printed in China by R.R. Donnelley

Front cover photograph by Ken Burris | Turkish Pasta with Bison Sauce (*page 47*)
This page | Ravioli & Vegetable Soup (*page 28*)

10 9 8 7 6 5 4 3 2 1

AUTHORS | Jessie Price & the EatingWell Test Kitchen
ASSOCIATE EDITOR | Carolyn Malcoun
TEST KITCHEN MANAGER | Stacy Fraser
TEST KITCHEN | Hilary Meyer (Assistant Editor),
Katie Webster (recipe developer, food stylist), Carolyn Casner (recipe tester),
Patsy Jamieson (food stylist), Susan Herr (food stylist)

ART DIRECTOR | Michael J. Balzano
PHOTOGRAPHER | Ken Burris
PRODUCTION DESIGNER | Beth Alessi
PRODUCTION ASSISTANCE | Amanda McAllister

MANAGING EDITOR | Wendy S. Ruopp
ASSISTANT MANAGING EDITOR | Alesia Depot
PRODUCTION MANAGER | Jennifer B. Brown
DEPUTY EDITOR: FEATURES & NUTRITION | Nicci Micco
DIETITIAN & NUTRITION ADVISOR | Sylvia Geiger, M.S., R.D.
CONTRIBUTING WRITER | Jim Romanoff
RESEARCH EDITOR | Anne Bliss
RESEARCH ASSISTANCE | Caroline H. Gottesman, Georgia S. Wright-Simmons
INDEXER | Amy Novick, BackSpace Indexing

EatingWell Media Group
CEO | Tom Witschi
EDITORIAL DIRECTOR | Lisa Gosselin

TABLE OF CONTENTS

40 WAYS TO SAVE MONEY, YOUR WAISTLINE AND YOUR HEALTH

BY JESSIE PRICE

What foods you eat have a huge impact on two very important bottom lines—your health and your wallet. Here at EATINGWELL we've always focused on making sure our recipes are good for you and delicious too. But we also want to make sure healthy eating is affordable for everyone. So we recently began calculating what it costs to make each of our recipes.

It quickly became clear that the first, easiest way to start saving is to cook at home. When you cook using whole, natural ingredients it's actually easy to make dinner for less than $3 a serving. And that's almost always cheaper than if you eat out. Sure the dollar "value" menu at a fast-food joint is an exception, but think about the impact it has on your health and your waistline. According to the USDA, eating fast food frequently can contribute to weight gain. Plus going out isn't quite as quick and easy as it's cracked up to be. Say you skip the fast food and go to a sit-down restaurant. Perhaps it takes 10 minutes to drive to the restaurant, you spend an hour at the restaurant and then you drive home another 10 minutes. You've just spent an hour and 20 minutes, plus you paid for gas. Even when you call for delivery, it's not all that fast. Maybe it takes 30 minutes for a pizza to arrive. But in the same amount of time you could make any of the recipes in this book that take less than 30 minutes to prepare.

The kicker is that cooking at home is almost always healthier too. Home-cooked meals are more likely to have reasonable serving sizes. Plus you can limit unhealthy ingredients like butter, salt and cream that are always big players in restaurant meals. And cooking at home has other less tangible benefits. Study after study has shown that kids who sit down to dinner with their family frequently are less likely to drink, smoke, do drugs or have eating disorders. And those kids are usually eating more fruits and vegetables, less fried food and soda, less saturated and trans fat and more fiber.

Whether you want to save money, improve your health, lose weight or just get your family together, EATINGWELL recipes are an amazing tool. We've had a lot of practice making great-tasting, healthy, easy recipes at EATINGWELL. But once we started digging into the costs it added a whole new angle to our recipe development. In the Test Kitchen we got pretty geeky about it...and even a little competitive. We wanted to see who could make the most delicious recipe and still have it cost less than $3 per serving. We came up with recipes like Maple-Chili Glazed Pork Medallions (*page 132*) and Crispy Chicken Tostadas (*page 84*) that you'll find in this book. We were thrilled with how well we could eat for cheap.

But to really put this book to the test we wanted to see how much we could cut the grocery bills for a family of four. So we devised an experiment: we shopped for and cooked a week's worth of regular EATINGWELL dinners and a week's worth of recipes from this book. (The chart at right shows you what we cooked and how much each meal cost.) We saved $52.35 for one week of dinners. Over a year, that works out to $2,722.20 of savings. Were we feeling deprived during our week of "budget" recipes? No way! Both weeks we ate delicious, satisfying, healthy dinners. But at about half the price, the budget week was hard to beat.

Of course we know that to really make this work we need to take real lives into account. Most of us don't actually cook dinner at home seven nights a week. Often we have evening commitments or eat leftovers. Also, we know that the amount we spend on a recipe can be quite different depending on where we shop, what season it is (think of the

Here's the EATINGWELL Test Kitchen team: Katie Webster, Jessie Price, Carolyn Malcoun (*in front*), Stacy Fraser, Hilary Meyer and Carolyn Casner (*in back*). They're responsible for making sure EATINGWELL recipes are easy, delicious and healthy. And the team loves the challenge of making great-tasting food that's affordable too.

REGULAR EATINGWELL WEEK	
Recipe (4 servings)	**Cost**
Pan-Seared Scallops with Sautéed Cucumbers	**15.19**
Grilled Lamb Chops with Eggplant Salad	**19.87**
Cod with Tomato Cream Sauce	**15.06**
Chicken & Sun-Dried Tomato Orzo	**16.26**
Steak & Potato Kebabs with Creamy Cilantro Sauce	**18.02**
Sautéed Chicken Breasts with Creamy Chive Sauce	**8.91**
Greek Orzo Stuffed Peppers	**16.62**
	$109.93

EATINGWELL ON A BUDGET WEEK	
Recipe (4 servings)	**Cost**
Louisiana Catfish with Okra & Corn (*p. 138*)	**9.03**
Pork Chops au Poivre (*p. 127*)	**6.77**
Sweet-&-Sour Chicken Drumsticks (*p. 90*)	**5.47**
Beef & Cabbage Stir-Fry w/ Peanut Sauce (*p. 117*)	**9.96**
Cheese-&-Spinach-Stuffed Portobellos (*p. 75*)	**6.59**
Salmon Rösti (*p. 148*)	**10.86**
Black Bean Croquettes with Fresh Salsa (*p. 79*)	**8.90**
	$57.58

price of raspberries in February) and all sorts of other factors. So there's more to it than just following the recipes (though that's a good start). We actually need to look for other ways to save money throughout the process, from shopping to storing to figuring out what to do when you're staring into the bottom of the produce drawer at a bell pepper that's a little past its prime. Here are our tips and techniques to make easy, healthy, delicious food and save money at the same time.

GET ORGANIZED

The first step to saving money is to avoid waste. Americans throw out more than 25 percent of the food we prepare, according to the Environmental Protection Agency. That means we need to do a better job of using leftovers, learn what to do with food when it's past its peak and most of all get organized. Here are some easy steps to take:

1. Make a game plan.
Start by being realistic about how many meals you'll cook at home in a week. Do you have other plans? Want to eat leftovers for lunch? Next, decide what you want to eat that week. If it's a busy week, try cooking a double batch of something on a night when you have more time to cook.

2. Not a planner?
Some of us don't love to plan meals in advance. If that's the case then just pick some of the main ingredients. For in-

stance you may want to roast a chicken one night and then make soup with the leftovers another night. Maybe you're longing for pizza another night and something with ground beef another. That's the start of a game plan.

3. Eat vegetarian a few nights a week.
Try to include a couple of vegetarian meals in your menu for the week. Skipping meat, even once or twice a week, can help save money, since meat is usually the most expensive part of a meal. And you will have a lighter impact on the environment—almost one-fifth of the world's man-made greenhouse-gas emissions are generated by the meat industry, according to the United Nations.

4. Try going almost meatless.
Plan meals where meat is used as a flavoring as opposed to being the central part of a meal. Just think about how most cultures around the world use meat—from Chinese chow mein to Italian pasta—and you get the picture. For instance, have a little sausage on a pizza or a bit of turkey along with plenty of vegetables in a panini.

5. Plan for what's in season.
Avoid choosing something like fresh asparagus in January, because that's when you'll pay big bucks for it (not to mention that it won't taste like much anyway). Instead, in the dead of winter opt for cauliflower or chard. Of course once you get to the store you may see something that looks great and is on sale, so be flexible enough to change your plans once you get there.

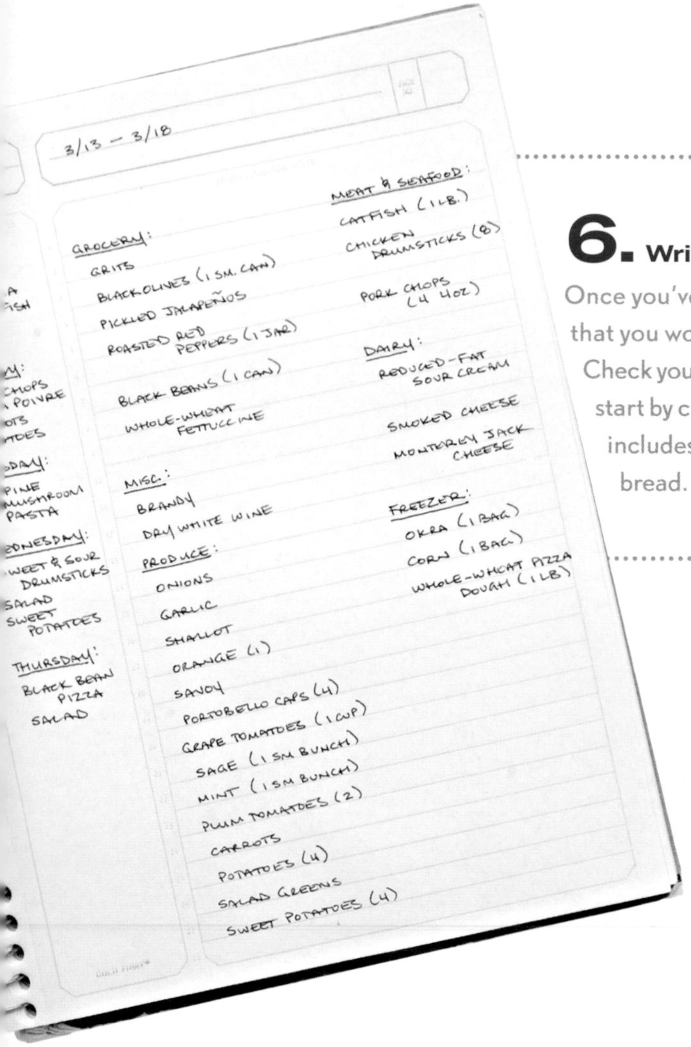

Handwritten shopping list (spiral notebook):

```
3/13 - 3/18

GROCERY:                    MEAT & SEAFOOD:
GRITS                       CATFISH (1 LB)
BLACK OLIVES (1 SM. CAN)    CHICKEN DRUMSTICKS (8)
PICKLED JALAPEÑOS
ROASTED RED PEPPERS (1 JAR) PORK CHOPS (4 4OZ)

BLACK BEANS (1 CAN)         DAIRY:
WHOLE-WHEAT FETTUCCINE      REDUCED-FAT SOUR CREAM
                            SMOKED CHEESE
MISC:                       MONTEREY JACK CHEESE
BRANDY
DRY WHITE WINE              FREEZER:
PRODUCE:                    OKRA (1 BAG)
ONIONS                      CORN (1 BAG)
GARLIC                      WHOLE-WHEAT PIZZA DOUGH (1 LB)
SHALLOT
ORANGE (1)
SAVOY
PORTOBELLO CAPS (4)
GRAPE TOMATOES (1 CUP)
SAGE (1 SM BUNCH)
MINT (1 SM BUNCH)
PLUM TOMATOES (2)
CARROTS
POTATOES (4)
SALAD GREENS
SWEET POTATOES (4)
```

(Partially visible left edge of meal plan):
... FISH ... CHOPS ... POIVRE ... TOES ... DAY: ... PINE MUSHROOM PASTA ... WEDNESDAY: SWEET & SOUR DRUMSTICKS ... SALAD SWEET POTATOES ... THURSDAY: BLACK BEAN PIZZA SALAD

6. Write a shopping list.

Once you've got a plan, it's time to make a list. That's the best insurance that you won't spend extra dollars on ingredients you don't really need. Check your recipes to see what you'll need to buy for the week. Get a head start by creating a list on your computer (in a spreadsheet program) that includes all the items you buy on a weekly basis, such as eggs, milk and bread. Then just print it out and add to it what you need.

SHOP SMART

Being prepared before heading to the store is the best way to make sure you spend your money well. But there are also some strategies to keep in mind and ingredients to keep an eye out for at the store. Here are some of our favorite ways to save while shopping.

9. Shop the club stores.

Club stores, such as Costco and Sam's Club, do have some great deals. For some of us (especially those with space in the house to store things like giant packages of toilet paper) the up-front membership fee pays for itself in no time. Two things to keep in mind when you shop at these stores: don't go overboard and don't always assume that you're getting a better deal at the club store. Do a little research before you shop and compare prices per weight to those in regular stores. Go in with a plan to avoid overpurchasing. We like to stock up on boxed broth, olive oil, frozen fish, canned tomatoes and nuts (to keep in the freezer). Be careful about buying produce at these stores. Only buy it if you're sure you can use it all up before it goes bad.

10. Eat local.

Farmers' markets and grocery stores that carry local produce often have beautiful foods for top dollar. But there are some ways to eat locally and save money. Choose local fruits, vegetables and meats when they're at their peak and likely at the best price. Visit pick-your-own farms for better prices, especially when you buy in bulk. Pick more than you'll eat in the next few days and then freeze extras for later. (*See page 193 for a guide to freezing produce.*) Also, shop roadside farmstands, which sometimes have better prices. Try visiting your local farmers' market just before

7. Keep a well-stocked pantry.

A well-stocked pantry is the best way to resist the urge to go out on those nights when you're not sure what's for dinner. With a few basics you can probably pull together a healthy, tasty meal in the same amount of time it would take you to go out (and for less money, too!). So always check to see what staples need replenishing or just write them down on your shopping list as soon as you use something up. Besides basics like olive oil and flour, make sure to keep things like canned beans, pasta and canned tuna on hand so you can quickly create a delicious dinner. (*Turn to page 195 to see our full list of what to keep stocked in a healthy pantry.*)

8. Get out the scissors.

If you're a coupon clipper, great, go for it. But it's best to do it after you write that shopping list. That way you don't fall into the trap of buying things you don't really need just because you have a great coupon for them. Check supermarket websites for coupons too.

closing, when everyone's packing up—you may be able to bargain for some end-of-day specials.

11. Shop the ethnic markets and grocery store aisles.

Ethnic stores and grocery store sections are great places to find interesting ingredients. And they often have cheaper prices on items like seafood, beans and fresh vegetables.

12. Is organic worth it?

Yes, organic usually means more expensive. Our take: if you can afford it, great. If not, you may just want to focus on picking things on the "dirty dozen" list of most contaminated fruits and vegetables (*see page 194*) to buy organic. The bottom line: the most important thing to do is eat more fruits and vegetables, whether they're organic or conventionally grown.

13. Skip the prepackaged salad mix.

Sure, bagged salad mixes are convenient. And anything that makes it easier to eat your veggies is a good thing. But they're also expensive and can quickly go from perky to wilted to downright slimy. So try buying heads of lettuce (which often last longer in your crisper) and make your own mixes. Try mixing up romaine, radicchio, red leaf and/or escarole. (*For salad ideas, see page 158.*)

14. Grow your own.

Another option for salad greens is to grow your own—they don't take up much space and they grow quickly. (*Turn to page 194 for how to get started growing greens.*) For about the cost of a bag of salad greens ($3) you can buy a packet of seeds for mixed salad greens. The packets have 500 seeds and will plant a 30-foot long row of greens. (We're not sure exactly how many salads that translates into, but it's safe to say you'll be swimming in salads for weeks.)

15. Buy spices from the bulk bins.

Spices are one of the keys to keeping food both healthy and delicious, because when you use bold flavors you don't need as much fat. Look for a store that carries spices in bulk—the price per ounce is often less expensive. Plus you can buy a smaller amount, which helps you save in two ways: The up-front price is less. But perhaps more important, spices have a shelf life. After a year or two in your cupboard they just don't have as much flavor. So when you buy smaller amounts, you're less likely to have old spices sitting around that are ready for the trash can—a serious waste of money.

16. Bulk up when it makes sense.

Compare the price per weight for other bulk items (besides spices) to those in packages before you assume that the bulk section is always a better deal. Sometimes the bulk section

wins, sometimes not. Where we live, grains like oats, whole-wheat flour and brown rice are often cheaper in boxes as opposed to bulk. And pumpkins seeds and pistachios are cheaper in bulk while other nuts are more expensive.

17. Save on staples.

Stock up on staples, such as olive oil, nuts, pasta and canned beans, when they're on sale.

18. Love your potatoes.

Russet potatoes, which are a good source of fiber, potassium and vitamin C, are a great nutritional bang for your buck—they only cost about 30¢ apiece. And these babies are truly versatile. Try baking them, then stuffing them with beans, vegetables and salsa; mash them; slice and roast them; or turn them into hash browns for breakfast. (*For more ways to use potatoes, see page 164.*)

19. Get chicken-savvy.

Boneless, skinless chicken breasts are super-convenient and practically fat-free, but they're usually the most expensive way.to buy chicken. Buy breasts when they're on sale or, to save money, buy a whole chicken and roast or grill it. (Turn to pages 85 and 86 for recipes.) Use leftovers in soups, salads or sandwiches. Whole legs, drumsticks and thighs are also good bets if you don't have time to cut up a chicken.

p. 90

Sweet-&-Sour Chicken Drumsticks

p. 96

Chicken Thighs with Green Olive, Cherry & Port Sauce

p. 84

Crispy Chicken Tostadas

p. 89

Quick Roast Chicken & Root Vegetables

20. Don't skimp on flavor.

Fresh herbs are pricy. But as with spices, we would never say to skip them—they're key to making healthy food taste great. Look for combination packages of fresh herbs; they may be labeled "poultry mix" and typically contain a couple of different herbs, such as rosemary, thyme and marjoram. That way you get a bit of a few different herbs and you'll likely have less waste. Growing your own is another great option. In many areas you can grow hearty herbs like rosemary outdoors all year long. Though the flavors will be slightly different, you can replace fresh herbs in a recipe with dried. The rule of thumb is to follow a three-to-one fresh-to-dried ratio. So if a recipe calls for 1 tablespoon (i.e., 3 teaspoons) of fresh thyme, use 1 teaspoon of dried. Rosemary, oregano, sage and thyme are good bets when going from fresh to dry. Avoid making swaps with cilantro, parsley or chives as the dried herbs don't have much flavor.

21. Bulk up with beans.

At about 50¢ or less for a ½-cup serving of canned beans, you just can't go wrong. They're packed with fiber and protein. We always keep cans in the cupboard and whip them out to toss with salads, pasta, stir-fries, in soups or for an easy dip. Dried beans are even less expensive than canned. Cook a big batch (*turn to page 191 to learn how*) then freeze extras for when you're ready to use them in a recipe.

22. Know your whole grains.

Barley, brown rice and whole-wheat pasta are economical whole-grain choices. Shop around to find the best price on more expensive whole grains, such as quinoa and wild rice.

23. Ground beef is your friend.

Saving money is all about meatloaf. Just kidding. But really, meatloaf's reputation as a budget-friendly food is deserved because its main ingredient, ground beef, is inexpensive. And when you buy a lean grind, it's also healthy. Meatloaf is not the only inexpensive meal to make with ground beef. Some of our favorite ways to use it include Taco Salad (*page 24*) and Portobello & Beef Patty Melt (*page 114*).

24. Know the deals at the fish counter.

Studies show that eating seafood twice a week can reduce your risk of heart disease. So make seafood a part of your diet. We always swing by the fish counter to look for specials. Also keep in mind that your best bet may be to buy frozen fish. It's often less expensive, and you can defrost it when you're ready to use it so you know it's fresh.

25. Discover great ways to use canned fish.

Just like their fresh counterparts, canned salmon and tuna provide omega-3 fats, which help keep your heart healthy by lowering triglycerides and blood pressure. The difference is that they're usually significantly cheaper. But think beyond mayo and celery. Try giving tuna an Asian twist with Sesame Tuna Salad (*page 19*) or combine canned salmon with shredded potatoes for a quick Salmon Rösti (*page 148*).

26. Stock up on frozen vegetables.

We always keep frozen vegetables on hand for dinners when the produce drawer is looking a little bare. Frozen vegetables are nutritious because they're picked at the peak of ripeness and then frozen to seal in their nutrients. And a bonus: most of them don't have added sodium like canned vegetables often do. Plus they're relatively inexpensive, especially when compared with their "fresh" counterparts out of season.

27. Look for your favorite meats on sale.

Not only is your freezer great for frozen vegetables, it's also great because it lets you take advantage of low prices when you find them. Stock up on the meats you like when you find them on sale. Also buy extra fresh fruits and vegetables when they're in season and less expensive, then freeze them for later. (*See page 193 for tips on the best way to freeze fruits and vegetables.*)

GET COOKING

Once you've made your plan and gone shopping, it's time to roll up your sleeves in the kitchen. Get familiar with the best cooking techniques for inexpensive ingredients. Be prepared with clever ways to use leftovers or foods that are a bit past their prime. And, of course, know how to properly store leftovers and extra ingredients to avoid waste. Here are some tips to help you save on cooking.

28. Cook and serve the right portions.

According to nutrition experts, a healthy serving of cooked meat is 3 ounces. That's about 4 ounces raw. If you're eating meat for dinner aim for it to take up no more than one-quarter of your plate. Fill half the plate with vegetables and the final quarter with a whole grain. Eating less meat is better for your health and your budget.

29. Cook 'em low and slow.

Tougher cuts of beef and pork are a lot cheaper than steaks and chops (about $2 to $6 per pound for many cuts compared with $10 or more per pound for steaks), but no one wants to eat a piece of leather for dinner. The best way to cook tough cuts of meat: cook them low and slow, usually for 3 or more hours, often in liquid, to make them melt-in-your-mouth tender. Try Chinese Pork & Vegetable Hot Pot (*page 123*) or Oven Barbecued Brisket (*page 119*).

30. Bring out the roast.

Roasting a big piece of meat is an easy way to feed a crowd. Of course, a crown rib roast or beef tenderloin (unless your market is running an amazing special) isn't an economical choice. So choose cuts, such as leg of lamb, turkey breast or pork shoulder, and roast them. Your guests will never guess that Middle Eastern Roast Lamb with Tahini Sauce (*page 135*) costs less than $3 per serving.

p. 117

Beef & Cabbage Stir-Fry with Peanut Sauce

p. 48

Pork & Bok Choy Stir-Fry

p. 72

Vegetable Fried Rice

Szechuan Tofu & Green Bean Stir-Fry

31. Add pasta or rice.

Got a few vegetables or a little leftover meat? Maybe you have some fixings for a salad or a light soup, but it's not quite dinner. Pasta and rice are cheap, healthy pantry items that let you turn a few leftovers into a meal. Try quickly sautéing peppers and onions and toss them with noodles, herbs and a little cheese, or add rice into a vegetable soup to make it more satisfying.

32. Stir-fry for dinner.

Stir-frying with plenty of vegetables and just a little bit of meat is an obvious choice when you want to make a quick and healthy dinner. It's also very forgiving, so if you have a little extra onion or half a leftover zucchini you want to use up, just throw it in your stir-fry.

33. Cook once, eat twice.

We like to double recipes so that we can get ahead on our cooking and have a dinner or lunch ready for later. The added benefit is it helps use up ingredients that we bought for that recipe (a bunch of herbs, for instance). Recipes that freeze well, like Rich Chicken Stew (*page 94*), Oven Barbecued Brisket (*page 119*) and Hungarian Beef Goulash (*page 120*) are great ones to double. Also consider cooking an extra chicken or more meat than you need. The leftovers are great in soups, salads, quesadillas or hash later in the week.

34. Pack a lunch.

When you're making dinner, think about what you're going to eat for lunch tomorrow. If you're making a salad for dinner, make a little extra and put it in a container, undressed, for lunch the next day. And what about your leftovers from dinner? Is there a little extra chicken or maybe part of a can of beans? Toss that in with your lunch salad. Packing lunch is a great way to make sure you're not wasting any leftovers—and to help you eat healthy, save money and save time throughout the day. (*For more quick ideas for lunch, turn to page 186.*)

35. Feed yourself (not the birds) with stale bread.

Turn stale bread into croutons for salads or soups. Just toss cubes with oil and some seasonings and bake them. (*Turn to page 102 for a recipe.*) Or turn stale bread into breadcrumbs to use in recipes like Black Bean Croquettes with Fresh Salsa (*page 79*) or Stuffed Tomatoes with Golden Crumb Topping (*page 112*). Turn to page 198 to learn how to make your own.

36. Hold onto brown bananas.

Freeze overripe bananas (peeled) if you don't have time to use them immediately. Throw them into smoothies (*see page 185*) or defrost them when you want to make some banana bread or muffins.

37. Squeeze your lemons.

We like to keep citrus on hand because it's a great way to perk up a sauce or a salad dressing. Keep lemons and limes in the refrigerator and if they start to get dried, shriveled or have brown spots on the skin, squeeze the juice and store it covered in the refrigerator or freezer.

GET EQUIPPED

You don't need fancy tools to cook and eat well for less. As in any kitchen, we recommend having the basics: sharp knives, kitchen shears, several cutting boards, stainless-steel pots and pans, a large nonstick skillet and so forth. Besides the basics, there are a few kitchen tools that may cost you something initially but will help you save money in the long run.

38. Seal it up.

Yes, it sounds like hyperbole, but vacuum-sealing tools are truly revolutionary when it comes to preserving food in the freezer. They ensure that your food—leftovers, meats, fruits, vegetable or extra stuff you bought in bulk—stays delicious, without freezer burn, for months.

39. Keep it fresh.

Make sure you have sealable storage containers on hand to save leftovers. You can buy inexpensive clear plastic or glass ones at the supermarket. When they're clear you can tell what's in them at a glance, and may be more likely to eat the leftovers.

Now that you know some of our favorite tricks to eating well and saving money, it's time to put it all into practice. Start planning by turning to the following chapters full of delicious, healthy recipes. You'll find main-course soups and salads, a chapter full of pizza, pasta and sandwiches, then vegetarian, poultry, meat and seafood chapters. There are ideas for simple sides, and don't forget the sweets! Plus in the Budget Basics chapter, you'll get some great ideas for snacks, lunches and breakfasts as well as some money-saving techniques, such as making your own chicken broth and fruit preserves. So get cooking, eat well and enjoy!

40. Plug in the slow cooker.

If you don't have hours to be at home tending a braise on the stove, try a slow cooker. It will give you the same effect (i.e., it gets tough, inexpensive cuts of meat meltingly tender), but you can plug it in, leave for the day and come home to a dinner like Rich Chicken Stew, below (*page 94*), or Hungarian Beef Goulash (*page 120*). Look for used slow cookers at garage sales or make the investment in a new one that is programmable and will automatically switch to a "keep warm" setting when it's done cooking. They start at about $40.

p. 95

Chicken & Sweet Potato Stew

p. 120

Hungarian Beef Goulash

p. 78

Barley Risotto with Fennel

p. 123

Chinese Pork & Vegetable Hot Pot

HEALTHIER FOOD, HAPPIER LIVES

How one group is changing lives, one healthy cooking lesson at a time

Healthy food should be accessible to everyone, no matter what their income. Unfortunately that's not always the case. The highest obesity rates in the U.S. are associated with the lowest incomes and education levels, according to a survey by the Centers for Disease Control and Prevention. Dr. Adam Drewnowski, professor of epidemiology at the University of Washington, says, "Simply put, fats and sweets cost less, whereas many healthier foods cost more."

Fortunately for some, like Yakeline Argueta, there are organizations working to reverse the link between obesity and low income. A native of El Salvador, Argueta fled her homeland to escape an abusive situation when she was 15 years old, leaving behind an infant daughter. "The man who abused me was trying to kill me," she says. Penniless, she hitchhiked her way first to Mexico and then to Canada to find work.

She eventually married and moved to the Washington, D.C., area, where she signed up with Linkages to Learning, a local nonprofit program that aids at-risk families. Linkages to Learning connected her with one of its affiliates, Through The Kitchen Door (TTKD). She enrolled as a student in TTKD's Healthy Family Kitchen 101 class, a 15-hour course that teaches basic kitchen techniques and how to cook healthy inexpensive food. But the goals of the class go way beyond simply teaching cooking skills. According to TTKD president and founder Liesel Flashenberg, "Our goal is to teach life

Yakeline Argueta

skills, self-confidence and professionalism to the people who need it most: low-income adults, at-risk youth and recent immigrants. We want to empower our students."

Argueta is one of TTKD's many success stories. When she started with them she was nearly 100 pounds overweight and had no formal culinary training. She graduated from the class a changed woman. She then lost more than 70 pounds and had the cooking savvy to feed her family well on a budget. "Now we eat vegetables, which we never ate before," she says. "Now my kids eat carrots instead of potato chips. We stopped drinking sodas. And we don't eat fast food anymore. Now I bulk-cook food with my children one day a week, so I save time and money."

Benefits, yes, but Argueta's greatest lesson learned has been self-respect. "Before I came here to Through The Kitchen Door," she says, "I didn't think I was deserving of any responsible job." To underscore her life change, Argueta now works with TTKD as a teacher and caterer and serves on the TTKD board of directors.

TTKD has expanded its programs during its 10 years in the D.C. metro area. It started out with a series of cooking and skills classes for low-income immigrant women. Today it includes an after-school program that teaches teens how to cook for themselves and become cost-conscious consumers. In the Commercial Kitchen 101 class, students learn how to become professional cooks. And TTKD even runs a catering business that gives students on-the-job training plus pay. To date, Flashenberg says, TTKD has trained and helped more than 2,500 adults and teens. Plans are under way for replicating the programs nationally and internationally.
—*Alexandra Greeley*

SALADS & SOUPS FOR DINNER

Don't just think of them as sides: adding plenty of vegetables, some grains and lean protein to soups and salads turns them into satisfying dinners. Plus they're a great way to use up what's in your fridge. Try adding leftovers—cooked potatoes, rice or chicken are excellent choices—to your greens or soup to make it a meal.

Chicken & Fruit Salad (*page 18*)

ACTIVE TIME: 15 minutes

TOTAL: 15 minutes

PER SERVING:

248 calories; 11 g fat (4 g sat, 2 g
mono); 55 mg cholesterol; 18 g
carbohydrate; 21 g protein; 4 g fiber;
346 mg sodium; 371 mg potassium.

NUTRITION BONUS:

Vitamin A (140% daily value), Vitamin
C (50% dv).

H✂W   H♥H

Chicken & Fruit Salad

Chicken, melon, walnuts and feta top mixed salad greens for a refreshing summer salad. This is a fine way to use up leftover grilled chicken breast or even sliced pork chops or tenderloin. Swap in your favorite summer fruit in place of the melon if you wish. (Photograph: page 16.)

¼ cup reduced-fat sour cream
3 tablespoons fruit-flavored vinegar
4 teaspoons sugar
1½ teaspoons poppy seeds
¼ teaspoon salt
    Freshly ground pepper to taste
8 cups mixed salad greens
2 cups sliced cooked chicken breast (*see Note, page 200*)
2 cups chopped melon, such as cantaloupe *and/or* honeydew
¼ cup chopped walnuts, toasted (*see Note, page 199*)
¼ cup crumbled feta cheese

Whisk sour cream, vinegar, sugar, poppy seeds, salt and pepper in a large bowl until smooth. Reserve ¼ cup of the dressing in a small bowl. Add the mixed greens to the large bowl and toss to coat. Divide among 4 plates and top with chicken, melon, walnuts and feta. Drizzle each portion with 1 tablespoon of the reserved dressing.

MAKES 4 SERVINGS.

Sesame Tuna Salad

Toasted sesame oil transforms a humble staple like canned tuna into an elegant supper. We love the crunch of napa cabbage in this salad, but plain romaine lettuce would also work if you happen to have that on hand.

ACTIVE TIME: 25 minutes

TOTAL: 25 minutes

PER SERVING.

228 calories; 16 g fat (2 g sat, 9 g mono); 12 mg cholesterol; 9 g carbohydrate; 14 g protein; 3 g fiber; 353 mg sodium; 199 mg potassium.

NUTRITION BONUS:

Vitamin C (80% daily value), Vitamin A (37% dv).

¼	cup rice vinegar *or* lemon juice
3	tablespoons canola oil
2	tablespoons reduced-sodium soy sauce
1	tablespoon toasted sesame oil
1½	teaspoons sugar
1½	teaspoons minced fresh ginger
2	5- to 6-ounce cans water-packed chunk light tuna, drained
1	cup sliced sugar snap peas *or* snow peas
2	scallions, sliced
6	cups thinly sliced napa cabbage
4	radishes, julienne-cut *or* sliced
¼	cup fresh cilantro leaves
1	tablespoon sesame seeds
	Freshly ground pepper to taste

1. Whisk vinegar (or lemon juice), canola oil, soy sauce, sesame oil, sugar and ginger in a small bowl.

2. Combine 3 tablespoons of the dressing, tuna, peas and scallions in a medium bowl.

3. Divide cabbage among 4 plates. Mound one-fourth of the tuna mixture (about ½ cup) in the center of each plate and garnish with radishes, cilantro and sesame seeds. Drizzle with the remaining dressing (about 2 tablespoons per salad) and season with pepper.

MAKES 4 SERVINGS.

Spicy Shrimp Salad

Cooked shrimp are always a crowd pleaser, plus they are an excellent source of lean protein. In this colorful salad they are tossed in a spicy Thai dressing with colorful bell pepper, cucumber and fresh herbs. Serve in Bibb lettuce cups as a light supper with a cup of pea soup (see page 156) or as an appetizer.

2	tablespoons lime juice
4	teaspoons fish sauce (*see Note*)
1	tablespoon canola oil
2	teaspoons light brown sugar
½	teaspoon crushed red pepper
1	pound cooked and peeled small shrimp
1	cup thinly sliced red, yellow *and/or* orange bell pepper
1	cup seeded and thinly sliced cucumber
¼	cup chopped mixed fresh herbs, such as basil, cilantro *and/or* mint

Whisk lime juice, fish sauce, oil, brown sugar and crushed red pepper in a large bowl. Add shrimp, bell pepper, cucumber and herbs; toss to coat.

MAKES 4 SERVINGS.

ACTIVE TIME: 15 minutes

TOTAL: 15 minutes

PER SERVING:

172 calories; 5 g fat (1 g sat, 2 g mono); 221 mg cholesterol; 6 g carbohydrate; 25 g protein; 1 g fiber; 651 mg sodium; 314 mg potassium.

NUTRITION BONUS:

Vitamin C (60% daily value), Vitamin A (25% dv), Iron (21% dv).

H✻W   H♥H

NOTE:

Fish sauce is a pungent condiment made from salted, fermented fish. Find it in the Asian section of large supermarkets and in Asian specialty markets. We use Thai Kitchen fish sauce, lower in sodium than other brands (1,190 mg per tablespoon), in our nutritional analyses

····SAVE····························

Purchase shrimp individually quick-frozen (IQF) in 2- to 5-pound bags. You can grab just what you need out of the bag and thaw them in minutes under cold running water.

ACTIVE TIME: 30 minutes

TOTAL: 50 minutes

TO MAKE AHEAD: Cover and refrigerate the vinaigrette (Step 1) for up to 1 week.

PER SERVING:

444 calories; 18 g fat (5 g sat, 10 g mono); 17 mg cholesterol; 56 g carbohydrate; 18 g protein; 12 g fiber; 579 mg sodium; 630 mg potassium.

NUTRITION BONUS:

Vitamin A (26% daily value), Vitamin C (25% dv), Iron (24% dv), Calcium & Potassium (18% dv).

H↑F H♥H

NOTE:

French green lentils are firmer than brown lentils and cook more quickly. They can be found in natural-foods stores and some supermarkets.

⋯⋯ SAVE ⋯⋯⋯⋯⋯⋯

Look for economical bottles of lemon juice at your market. They contain at least a dozen lemons' worth of high-quality juice for around $3. Look for brands that list just lemon juice on the ingredient label.

Couscous, Lentil & Arugula Salad with Garlic-Dijon Vinaigrette

This hearty combination of whole-wheat couscous and lentils perched atop a lightly dressed bed of arugula makes a tasty vegetarian main-course salad. The lemony vinaigrette is especially good for bringing out the spicy notes of the arugula. This recipe makes a large batch of dressing—more than you'll need for this salad. We love to have the leftovers on hand to dress salads later in the week.

VINAIGRETTE
- ½ cup extra-virgin olive oil
- ½ cup lemon juice
- ½ cup red-wine vinegar
- ¼ cup Dijon mustard
- 4 small cloves garlic, minced
- ½ teaspoon salt
   Freshly ground pepper to taste

SALAD
- 1¼ cups vegetable broth *or* water
- 1 cup whole-wheat couscous
- 2½ cups water
- 1 cup French green lentils (*see Note*) *or* brown lentils, rinsed
- 4 cups arugula, any tough stems removed, *or* mixed salad greens
- 1 small cucumber, peeled, seeded and diced
- 1 cup cherry tomatoes, halved
- ½ cup crumbled feta cheese

1. **To prepare vinaigrette:** Combine oil, lemon juice, vinegar, mustard and garlic in a blender, a jar with a tight-fitting lid or a medium bowl. Blend, shake or whisk until smooth. Season with salt and pepper.

2. **To prepare salad:** Bring 1¼ cups broth (or water) to a boil in a small saucepan. Add couscous, cover, remove from the heat and let stand until the liquid is absorbed, about 5 minutes.

3. Combine 2½ cups water and lentils in another saucepan. Bring to a boil, reduce heat to a simmer, cover and cook until just tender, 15 to 25 minutes. (Green lentils will be done sooner than brown lentils.) Be careful not to overcook the lentils or they will fall apart in the salad. Drain any excess water and let cool for about 10 minutes.

4. If arugula leaves are large, tear into bite-size pieces. Toss arugula (or greens) with ¼ cup of the vinaigrette in a large bowl, then divide among 4 large plates. In the same bowl, toss the couscous and lentils with another ¼ cup vinaigrette; divide the mixture among the plates. Top each salad with cucumber, tomatoes and feta and drizzle each with 1 tablespoon vinaigrette. (Cover and refrigerate the remaining 1 cup vinaigrette for up to 1 week.)

MAKES 4 SERVINGS, ABOUT 2 CUPS EACH.

ACTIVE TIME: 30 minutes

TOTAL: 30 minutes

PER SERVING:

447 calories; 19 g fat (8 g sat, 5 g mono); 108 mg cholesterol; 27 g carbohydrate; 42 g protein; 10 g fiber; 620 mg sodium; 1,124 mg potassium.

NUTRITION BONUS:

Vitamin A (184% daily value), Vitamin C (53% dv), Zinc (51% dv), Folate (48% dv), Iron (33% dv), Potassium (32% dv), Calcium (22% dv), Magnesium (20% dv).

H ⬆ F

Taco Salad

A super-quick blend of reduced-fat sour cream and salsa serves double duty as salad dressing and seasoning for the meat in our updated version of a Tex-Mex taco salad. Depending on the type of salsa you use, the salad will vary in heat. Hold the deep-fried tortilla bowl and instead serve this salad with baked Chile-Lime Tortilla Chips (page 188) and wedges of fresh lime.

½   cup prepared salsa
¼   cup reduced-fat sour cream
1   teaspoon canola oil
1   medium onion, chopped
3   cloves garlic, minced
1   pound 93%-lean ground beef *or* turkey
2   large plum tomatoes, diced
1   14-ounce can kidney beans, rinsed
2   teaspoons ground cumin
2   teaspoons chili powder
¼   cup chopped fresh cilantro
8   cups shredded romaine lettuce
½   cup shredded sharp Cheddar cheese

1. Combine salsa and sour cream in a large bowl.

2. Heat oil in a large nonstick skillet over medium heat. Add onion and garlic and cook, stirring often, until softened, about 2 minutes. Add beef (or turkey) and cook, stirring often and crumbling with a wooden spoon, until cooked through, about 5 minutes. Add tomatoes, beans, cumin and chili powder; cook, stirring, until the tomatoes begin to break down, 2 to 3 minutes. Remove from the heat, stir in cilantro and ¼ cup of the salsa mixture.

3. Add lettuce to the remaining salsa mixture in the bowl; toss to coat. To serve, divide the lettuce among 4 plates, top with the meat mixture and sprinkle with cheese.

MAKES 4 SERVINGS (1 CUP FILLING & 2 CUPS SALAD EACH).

Curried Red Lentil Soup

This soup is inspired by the Indian side dish dal; *the Hindi word means "split" and refers to the split peas or lentils used in its preparation. Fragrant ginger, curry, cinnamon and cumin add lots of rich flavor. Shop at your local natural-foods market for lentils and spices in bulk and get the freshest ingredients for the best prices.*

1	tablespoon canola oil
1	large onion, chopped
3	cloves garlic, minced
2	tablespoons minced fresh ginger
1	jalapeño pepper, seeded and minced
1½	tablespoons curry powder
1½	teaspoons ground cinnamon
1	teaspoon ground cumin
2	bay leaves
1½	cups red lentils, rinsed and picked over (*see Notes*)
8	cups reduced-sodium chicken broth
3	tablespoons chopped fresh cilantro *or* parsley
2	tablespoons lemon juice
	Freshly ground pepper to taste
⅓	cup nonfat plain yogurt
2	tablespoons prepared mango chutney (optional; *see Notes*)

1. Heat oil in a Dutch oven over medium heat. Add onion and cook, stirring occasionally, until softened, 3 to 5 minutes. Add garlic, ginger, jalapeno, curry powder, cinnamon, cumin and bay leaves and cook, stirring often, for about 5 minutes more.

2. Stir in lentils and broth and bring to a boil. Reduce heat to low and simmer, partially covered, until the lentils are tender, about 45 minutes.

3. Discard bay leaves. Stir in cilantro (or parsley) and lemon juice. Season with pepper. Ladle the soup into bowls and garnish with yogurt and chutney (if using).

MAKES 6 SERVINGS, ABOUT 1½ CUPS EACH.

ACTIVE TIME: 25 minutes

TOTAL: 55 minutes

PER SERVING:

231 calories; 3 g fat (0 g sat, 2 g mono); 0 mg cholesterol; 36 g carbohydrate; 18 g protein; 13 g fiber; 753 mg sodium; 875 mg potassium.

NUTRITION BONUS:

Folate (68% daily value), Iron (32% dv), Potassium (25% dv), Vitamin C (17% dv), Magnesium (15% dv).

H✳W   H↑F   H♥H

NOTES:

Red lentils are a useful addition to your pantry because they cook in just 10 to 15 minutes. They are excellent in soups, salads and vegetarian stews. You can find them in the natural-foods section of your supermarket or in natural-foods stores.

Look for **mango chutney** in the Indian section of the supermarket.

····· S A V E ······························

Not sure what else to do with mango chutney? Whisk some with yogurt for a quick dressing, dip or marinade. Or serve with grilled meat, fish or chicken.

Sweet Potato-Peanut Bisque

This satisfying vegetarian sweet potato soup is inspired by the flavors of West African peanut soup. We like the added zip of hot green chiles, but you can use mild chiles if you prefer. Serve with a mixed green salad with vinaigrette.

2   large sweet potatoes (10-12 ounces each)
1   tablespoon canola oil
1   small yellow onion, chopped
1   large clove garlic, minced
3   cups reduced-sodium tomato-vegetable juice blend *or* tomato juice
1   4-ounce can diced green chiles, preferably hot, drained
2   teaspoons minced fresh ginger
1   teaspoon ground allspice
1   15-ounce can vegetable broth
½   cup smooth natural peanut butter
     Freshly ground pepper to taste
     Chopped fresh cilantro leaves for garnish

1. Prick sweet potatoes in several places with a fork. Microwave on High until just cooked through, 7 to 10 minutes. Set aside to cool.

2. Meanwhile, heat oil in a large saucepan or Dutch oven over medium-high heat. Add onion and cook, stirring, until it just begins to brown, 2 to 4 minutes. Add garlic and cook, stirring, for 1 minute more. Stir in juice, green chiles, ginger and allspice. Adjust the heat so the mixture boils gently; cook for 10 minutes.

3. Peel the sweet potatoes and chop into bite-size pieces. Add half to the pan. Place the other half in a food processor or blender along with broth and peanut butter. Puree until completely smooth. Add the puree to the pan and stir well to combine. Thin the bisque with water, if desired. Season with pepper. Heat until hot. Garnish with cilantro, if desired.

MAKES 5 SERVINGS, ABOUT 1½ CUPS EACH.

ACTIVE TIME: 30 minutes

TOTAL: 30 minutes

TO MAKE AHEAD: Cover and refrigerate for up to 3 days. Thin with water before reheating, if desired.

PER SERVING:

291 calories; 16 g fat (3 g sat, 8 g mono); 0 mg cholesterol; 30 g carbohydrate; 10 g protein; 6 g fiber; 474 mg sodium; 1,011 mg potassium.

NUTRITION BONUS:

Vitamin A (300% daily value), Vitamin C (100% dv), Potassium (29% dv), Magnesium (15% dv).

H)(W   H↑F   H♥H

····SAVE····················

Try using your store's private-label brand ingredients, like tomato-vegetable juice in this recipe. Often they're just as good and cost a lot less than major national brands.

ACTIVE TIME: 25 minutes

TOTAL: 25 minutes

TO MAKE AHEAD: Cover and refrigerate for up to 3 days. Thin with broth before reheating, if desired.

PER SERVING:

264 calories; 9 g fat (3 g sat, 3 g mono); 28 mg cholesterol; 38 g carbohydrate; 11 g protein; 8 g fiber; 763 mg sodium; 762 mg potassium.

NUTRITION BONUS:

Vitamin C (60% daily value), Vitamin A (40% dv), Iron (21% dv), Calcium (16% dv).

H✖W   H⬆F   H❤H

Ravioli & Vegetable Soup

Fresh or frozen ravioli cook in minutes and turn this light vegetable soup into a main course. Look for whole-wheat or whole-grain ravioli in the refrigerated or frozen section of the supermarket. Tortellini can be used instead of ravioli as well. (Photograph: page 2.)

1	tablespoon extra-virgin olive oil
2	cups frozen bell pepper and onion mix, thawed and diced
2	cloves garlic, minced
¼	teaspoon crushed red pepper, or to taste (optional)
1	28-ounce can crushed tomatoes, preferably fire-roasted
1	15-ounce can vegetable broth *or* reduced-sodium chicken broth
1½	cups hot water
1	teaspoon dried basil *or* marjoram
1	6- to 9-ounce package fresh *or* frozen cheese (*or* meat) ravioli, preferably whole-wheat
2	cups diced zucchini (about 2 medium)
	Freshly ground pepper to taste

Heat oil in a large saucepan or Dutch oven over medium heat. Add pepper-onion mix, garlic and crushed red pepper (if using) and cook, stirring, for 1 minute. Add tomatoes, broth, water and basil (or marjoram); bring to a rolling boil over high heat. Add ravioli and cook for 3 minutes less than the package directions. Add zucchini; return to a boil. Cook until the zucchini is crisp-tender, about 3 minutes. Season with pepper.

MAKES 4 SERVINGS, ABOUT 2 CUPS EACH.

Amazon Bean Soup with Winter Squash & Greens

Buttercup squash most closely resembles the local squash used in this comforting hearty soup from northern Brazil, but you could certainly use hubbard, butternut, delicata or whichever orange-fleshed winter squash is on sale at the market.

1 tablespoon butter
4 cloves garlic, minced
2 carrots, chopped
1 medium onion, chopped
6 cups reduced-sodium chicken broth
3 pounds buttercup squash, peeled and diced (about 6 cups; *see Note*)
1 plum tomato, chopped
1/4 teaspoon crushed red pepper
1/4 teaspoon salt
1/8 teaspoon freshly ground pepper
2 15-ounce cans pinto *or* other brown beans, rinsed
10 ounces spinach, stemmed and coarsely chopped
1 lime, cut into wedges

1. Melt butter in a Dutch oven over medium-high heat. Add garlic, carrots and onion and cook, stirring occasionally, until the vegetables are tender and lightly browned, 5 to 7 minutes. Add broth and scrape up any browned bits with a wooden spoon. Add squash, tomato, crushed red pepper, salt and pepper and bring to a boil. Reduce heat to a simmer and cook until the squash is very soft and almost breaking apart, about 20 minutes.

2. Transfer 3 cups of the soup to a blender and puree until smooth. (Use caution when pureeing hot liquids.) Return the pureed soup to the pot. Stir in beans and spinach and cook over medium heat until the beans are heated through and the spinach is wilted, about 5 minutes. Serve with lime wedges.

MAKES 8 SERVINGS, 1 1/2 CUPS EACH.

ACTIVE TIME: 40 minutes

TOTAL: 1 hour 10 minutes

PER SERVING:

181 calories; 2 g fat (1 g sat, 0 g mono); 4 mg cholesterol; 34 g carbohydrate; 10 g protein; 8 g fiber; 618 mg sodium; 1,080 mg potassium.

NUTRITION BONUS:

Vitamin A (370% daily value), Vitamin C (60% dv), Folate (42% dv), Potassium (31% dv), Magnesium (24% dv), Iron (19% dv).

H❋W   H⬆F   H❤H

NOTE:

Fresh **winter squash** can be difficult to peel and cut. To soften the skin slightly, pierce squash in several places with a fork. Microwave on High for 45 to 60 seconds, heating it just long enough to slightly steam the skin, to make it easier to peel with a paring knife or vegetable peeler.

ACTIVE TIME: 30 minutes

TOTAL: 45 minutes

PER SERVING:

275 calories; 12 g fat (4 g sat, 4 g mono); 52 mg cholesterol; 24 g carbohydrate; 19 g protein; 5 g fiber; 759 mg sodium; 537 mg potassium.

NUTRITION BONUS:

Vitamin A (40% daily value), Iron, Potassium & Zinc (15% dv).

H❌W   H⬆F

NOTES:

Anaheim chiles (a.k.a. New Mexico chiles) are 7 to 10 inches long, ripen from green to red and are mildly spicy. **Poblano peppers** (sometimes called pasilla peppers) are dark green in color, about 6 inches long and can be fiery or relatively mild; there's no way to tell until you taste them. The two can be used interchangeably and are found at most large supermarkets.

To trim boneless, skinless **chicken thighs**, use kitchen shears to snip the fat away from the meat.

Tortilla Soup

Soup makes an inexpensive and filling lunch or light supper. Here's a version of chicken tortilla soup that's both super-easy and delicious. This is a great way to use up leftover tortillas. Even stale ones will be tasty once they're toasted. To make it even quicker, use crumbled tortilla chips in place of the homemade tortilla strips and skip Steps 1-2. Serve with vinegary coleslaw, lime wedges and hot sauce.

8	6-inch corn tortillas, halved and cut into strips
	Canola *or* olive oil cooking spray
1	tablespoon canola oil
3	Anaheim *or* poblano peppers (*see Notes*), diced
1	medium onion, diced
1	teaspoon ground cumin
1	pound boneless, skinless chicken thighs, trimmed and cut into 1-inch pieces (*see Notes*)
4	cups reduced-sodium chicken broth
1	14-ounce can diced tomatoes with green chiles
2	tablespoons lime juice
½	cup shredded sharp Cheddar cheese
¼	cup chopped fresh cilantro

1. Preheat oven to 400°F.

2. Spread tortilla strips in an even layer on a baking sheet and coat with cooking spray. Bake until browned and crispy, 12 to 15 minutes.

3. Meanwhile, heat oil in a large saucepan over medium heat. Add peppers and onion and cook, stirring, until the onion begins to soften, 3 to 5 minutes. Add cumin and cook, stirring, for 1 minute. Add chicken, broth, tomatoes and their juice; bring to a boil. Reduce heat and simmer until the chicken is cooked through, 12 to 15 minutes. Remove from the heat and stir in lime juice. Serve each portion topped with some of the baked tortilla strips, Cheddar and cilantro.

MAKES 6 SERVINGS, ABOUT 1 ⅓ CUPS EACH.

Cream of Turkey & Wild Rice Soup

It's almost impossible to make a turkey without leftovers and this recipe is a perfect way to use them up. It's a healthier twist on the classic creamy turkey and wild rice soup that hails from Minnesota. Of course, if you have leftover chicken, don't let that stop you—it'll work just fine. Serve with a crisp romaine salad and whole-grain bread.

1	tablespoon extra-virgin olive oil
2	cups sliced mushrooms (about 4 ounces)
3/4	cup chopped celery
3/4	cup chopped carrots
1/4	cup chopped shallots
1/4	cup all-purpose flour
1/4	teaspoon salt
1/4	teaspoon freshly ground pepper
4	cups reduced-sodium chicken broth
1	cup quick-cooking *or* instant wild rice (*see Note*)
3	cups shredded cooked turkey *or* chicken (*see Note, page 200*)
1/2	cup reduced-fat sour cream
2	tablespoons chopped fresh parsley

1. Heat oil in a large saucepan over medium heat. Add mushrooms, celery, carrots and shallots and cook, stirring, until softened, about 5 minutes. Add flour, salt and pepper and cook, stirring, for 2 minutes more.

2. Add broth and bring to a boil, scraping up any browned bits. Add rice and reduce heat to a simmer. Cover and cook until the rice is tender, 5 to 7 minutes. Stir in turkey (or chicken), sour cream and parsley and cook until heated through, about 2 minutes more.

MAKES 4 SERVINGS, ABOUT 1 3/4 CUPS EACH.

ACTIVE TIME: 35 minutes

TOTAL: 35 minutes

PER SERVING:

344 calories; 8 g fat (3 g sat, 4 g mono); 82 mg cholesterol; 27 g carbohydrate; 35 g protein; 3 g fiber; 792 mg sodium; 781 mg potassium.

NUTRITION BONUS:

Vitamin A (90% daily value), Potassium (22% dv), Zinc (20% dv), Folate & Iron (16% dv).

NOTE:

Conventional **wild rice** takes 40 to 50 minutes to cook. Quick-cooking or instant wild rice has been parboiled to reduce the cooking time. Be sure to check the cooking directions when selecting your rice—some brands labeled "quick" take about 30 minutes to cook. If you can't find the quick-cooking variety, just add cooked conventional wild rice along with the turkey in Step 2.

Sweet & Sour Beef-Cabbage Soup

ACTIVE TIME: 30 minutes

TOTAL: 30 minutes

This wholesome sweet-and-sour soup is a delicious way to turn a pound of ground beef into a filling meal for six. Caraway seeds, sweet paprika and cabbage give this dish an unmistakable German character. It is particularly nice served with crusty rye bread. For an even heartier soup, add diced cooked potatoes along with the cabbage.

PER SERVING:

250 calories; 10 g fat (3 g sat, 5 g mono); 54 mg cholesterol; 20 g carbohydrate; 20 g protein; 4 g fiber; 705 mg sodium; 717 mg potassium.

NUTRITION BONUS:

Vitamin C (45% daily value), Vitamin A (30% dv), Zinc (27% dv), Potassium (20% dv), Iron (19% dv).

H✳W   H♥H

NOTE:

Paprika specifically labeled as "Hungarian" delivers a fuller, richer flavor than regular or Spanish paprika. Find it at specialty-foods stores or online at *HungarianDeli.com* and *penzeys.com*.

1	tablespoon canola oil
1	pound lean (90% or leaner) ground beef
1½	teaspoons caraway seeds
1	teaspoon dried thyme
2½	cups frozen bell pepper and onion mix, thawed, chopped
1	medium Golden Delicious *or* other sweet-tart cooking apple, unpeeled, diced
6	cups reduced-sodium beef broth
1	15-ounce can crushed *or* diced tomatoes
1½	tablespoons honey
1	tablespoon paprika, preferably Hungarian sweet (*see Note*)
3	cups coarsely chopped Savoy *or* green cabbage
1-2	tablespoons cider vinegar
¼	teaspoon salt
	Freshly ground pepper to taste

1. Heat oil in a Dutch oven over medium heat. Add beef, caraway seeds and thyme and cook, stirring and breaking up the beef with a spoon, until it is mostly browned, about 4 minutes. Stir in pepper-onion mix and apple; cook, stirring, for 2 to 3 minutes more.

2. Stir in broth, tomatoes and their juice, honey and paprika and adjust the heat so the mixture boils gently. Cook for 8 to 10 minutes to blend the flavors. Stir in cabbage and cook just until barely tender, 3 to 4 minutes more. Season with vinegar to taste, salt and pepper.

MAKES 6 SERVINGS, ABOUT 1 ¾ CUPS EACH.

····SAVE····················

It's sometimes hard for a small family to eat a whole head of cabbage in one meal. Look for halved cabbages at the super-market. Or if you end up with leftovers, slice it thinly to make coleslaw or use it in a stir-fry like the Beef & Cabbage Stir-Fry with Peanut Sauce on page 117.

ACTIVE TIME: 30 minutes

TOTAL: 30 minutes

PER SERVING:

115 calories; 5 g fat (1 g sat, 2 g mono); 27 mg cholesterol; 4 g carbohydrate; 15 g protein; 2 g fiber; 552 mg sodium; 496 mg potassium.

NUTRITION BONUS:

Vitamin C (50% daily value), Vitamin A (25% dv), source of omega-3s.

H✖W H♥H

NOTE:

Instant mashed potato flakes is not a product that the EATINGWELL Test Kitchen typically uses, but we love how it gives creamy texture to soup without adding extra fat. Look for a brand that has the fewest ingredients possible (and therefore little to no artificial additives or flavoring). At our local market, the store brand was the best choice.

········SAVE········

If you buy fresh dill, or most any fresh herb for that matter, you can freeze extras, packed loosely in airtight containers, for several months with little negative effect on the flavor.

Salmon Chowder

Instant mashed potato flakes are the secret to giving this soup a thick, chowder texture without any heavy cream or butter. The flavor of the chowder is greatly enhanced by adding either fresh dill or dried tarragon.

1	tablespoon canola oil
⅓	cup chopped carrot
⅓	cup chopped celery
4	cups reduced-sodium chicken broth
1½	cups water
1	12-ounce skinned salmon fillet, preferably wild-caught (*see Note, page 200*)
2½	cups frozen cauliflower florets, thawed and coarsely chopped
3	tablespoons chopped fresh chives *or* scallions *or* 1½ tablespoons dried chives
1⅓	cups instant mashed potato flakes (*see Note*) *or* 2 cups leftover mashed potatoes
¼	cup chopped fresh dill *or* 2 teaspoons dried tarragon
1	tablespoon Dijon mustard
¼	teaspoon salt
	Freshly ground pepper to taste

1. Heat oil in a large saucepan or Dutch oven over medium heat. Add carrot and celery and cook, stirring frequently, until the vegetables just begin to brown, 3 to 4 minutes. Add broth, water, salmon, cauliflower and chives (or scallions) and bring to a simmer. Cover and cook, maintaining a gentle simmer, until the salmon is just cooked through, 5 to 8 minutes. Remove the salmon to a clean cutting board. Flake into bite-size pieces with a fork.

2. Stir potato flakes (or leftover mashed potatoes), dill (or tarragon) and mustard into the soup until well blended. Return to a simmer. Add the salmon and reheat. Season with salt and pepper.

MAKES 6 SERVINGS, ABOUT 1½ CUPS EACH.

PIZZA, PASTA & SANDWICHES

Pizza, pasta and sandwiches are some of the most popular, comforting dishes around. They provide a base of filling, fiber-rich grains—pizza dough, pasta and bread—that you can dress up with small amounts of pricier ingredients, such as meats, herbs and cheeses.

2

Sausage, Pepper & Mushroom Pizza (*page 40*)

ACTIVE TIME: 30 minutes

TOTAL: 40 minutes

PER SERVING:

275 calories; 6 g fat (3 g sat, 1 g mono); 28 mg cholesterol; 35 g carbohydrate; 16 g protein; 3 g fiber; 702 mg sodium; 248 mg potassium.

NUTRITION BONUS:

Vitamin C (33% daily value), Calcium (16% dv).

H⭑W   H♥H

NOTE:

Look for balls of whole-wheat **pizza dough**, fresh or frozen, at your supermarket. Or you may be able to buy them from your local pizza place. Choose a brand without hydrogenated oils. If you want to make your own, turn to page 191.

Sausage, Pepper & Mushroom Pizza

This is just a little more work than calling for delivery (but not by much), and there's no tipping required when you make it yourself. Plus you get it fresh from your oven, and with whole-wheat dough and a generous amount of vegetables on top it's far better for you. (Photograph: page 38.)

1	pound prepared pizza dough, preferably whole-wheat (*see Note*)
6	ounces Italian turkey sausage, about 2 large links, casings removed
1	green bell pepper, sliced
2	cups sliced mushrooms
¼	cup water
1	cup prepared marinara sauce *or* pizza sauce
1	cup shredded part-skim mozzarella cheese, preferably "fancy"

1. Position oven rack in the lowest position; preheat to 450°F. Coat a large baking sheet with cooking spray.

2. Roll out or stretch dough on a lightly floured surface to about the size of the baking sheet. Transfer to the baking sheet. Bake until puffed and lightly crisped on the bottom, 8 to 10 minutes.

3. Meanwhile, crumble sausage into a medium nonstick skillet. Cook over medium heat, breaking up with a spatula or spoon, until cooked through, 3 to 5 minutes. Place bell pepper, mushrooms and water in a large microwave-safe bowl. Cover and microwave on High until just tender, 3 to 4 minutes. Drain.

4. Spread sauce evenly over the crust. Top with the sausage, pepper and mushrooms and sprinkle with cheese. Bake until the crust is crispy and golden and the cheese is melted, 8 to 10 minutes.

MAKES 6 SERVINGS.

Thai Chicken Pizza

Today's pizzas have gone global—this Thai twist on pizza is a perfect example. Serve as is or with optional toppings, such as thinly sliced basil, cilantro, chopped peanuts and/or crushed red pepper on the side.

20   ounces prepared pizza dough, preferably whole-wheat (*see Note, page 40*)
¼   cup smooth natural peanut butter
3   tablespoons water
2   teaspoons reduced-sodium soy sauce
2   teaspoons rice vinegar
2   teaspoons minced fresh ginger
1   clove garlic, minced
1   teaspoon canola oil
8   ounces boneless, skinless chicken breast, trimmed and diced
1   red bell pepper, diced
4   scallions, thinly sliced
⅔   cup shredded part-skim mozzarella cheese

1. Place oven rack in the lowest position; preheat to 450°F. Coat a large baking sheet with cooking spray.

2. Roll out or stretch dough on a lightly floured surface to about the size of the baking sheet. Transfer to the baking sheet. Bake until puffed and lightly crisped on the bottom, 8 to 10 minutes.

3. Meanwhile, whisk peanut butter, water, soy sauce, vinegar, ginger and garlic in a small bowl until well combined.

4. Heat oil in a medium nonstick skillet over medium-high heat. Add chicken and cook, stirring, until cooked through, 2 to 4 minutes. Transfer to a medium bowl. Add bell pepper, scallions and 1 tablespoon of the peanut sauce to the chicken; toss to combine.

5. Spread the remaining peanut sauce evenly over the crust. Top with the chicken mixture and sprinkle with cheese. Bake until the crust is crispy and golden and the cheese is melted, 11 to 13 minutes.

MAKES 6 SERVINGS.

ACTIVE TIME: 35 minutes

TOTAL: 35 minutes

PER SERVING:

357 calories; 9 g fat (2 g sat, 1 g mono); 29 mg cholesterol; 41 g carbohydrate; 20 g protein; 3 g fiber; 431 mg sodium; 152 mg potassium.

NUTRITION BONUS:

Vitamin C (45% daily value), Vitamin A (15% dv).

H ♥ H

SAVE

Ordering pizza seems like a cheap and quick solution for dinner. But a typical pie costs about $15 before delivery. You can make your own at home for a lot less and in about the same amount of time delivery takes.

Green Pizza

Change up what you put on your pizza and try cooler-weather vegetables like broccoli and arugula as toppings. Arugula adds a slightly bitter, peppery taste, but you can use whichever greens are in season and the best buy at the market. For a milder flavor, swap in spinach or even chard for the arugula. Serve with a simple green salad.

ACTIVE TIME: 20 minutes

TOTAL: 30 minutes

PER SERVING:

323 calories; 13 g fat (4 g sat, 7 g mono); 19 mg cholesterol; 33 g carbohydrate; 15 g protein; 3 g fiber; 511 mg sodium; 241 mg potassium.

NUTRITION BONUS:

Vitamin C (45% daily value), Calcium (34% dv), Vitamin A (31% dv).

H✳W

1	pound prepared pizza dough, preferably whole-wheat (*see Note, page 199*)
2	cups chopped broccoli florets
¼	cup water
5	ounces arugula, any tough stems removed, chopped (about 6 cups)
	Pinch of salt
	Freshly ground pepper to taste
½	cup prepared pesto
1	cup shredded part-skim mozzarella cheese

1. Position oven rack in the lowest position; preheat to 450°F. Coat a large baking sheet with cooking spray.

2. Roll out or stretch dough on a lightly floured surface to about the size of the baking sheet. Transfer to the baking sheet. Bake until puffed and lightly crisped on the bottom, 8 to 10 minutes.

3. Meanwhile, cook broccoli and water in a large skillet over medium heat, covered, until the broccoli is crisp-tender, about 3 minutes. Stir in arugula and cook, stirring, until wilted, 1 to 2 minutes more. Season with salt and pepper.

4. Spread pesto evenly over the crust. Top with the broccoli mixture and sprinkle with cheese. Bake until the crust is crispy and golden and the cheese is melted, 8 to 10 minutes.

MAKES 6 SERVINGS.

SAVE

Store-bought pizza dough is convenient, but for less than a dollar, you can make your own dough, which takes only 20 minutes to prepare and keeps in the refrigerator for up to 1 day or in the freezer for up to 3 months. See our recipe for Easy Whole-Wheat Pizza Dough, page 191.

ACTIVE TIME: 40 minutes

TOTAL: 40 minutes

PER SERVING:

317 calories; 8 g fat (4 g sat, 2 g
mono); 17 mg cholesterol; 46 g
carbohydrate; 14 g protein; 7 g fiber;
692 mg sodium; 352 mg potassium.

NUTRITION BONUS:

Folate (35% daily value), Vitamin A
(20% dv), Calcium & Iron (19% dv).

H✕W H↑F

OVEN VARIATION:

Place a pizza stone on the lowest rack;
preheat oven to 450°F for at least 20
minutes. Roll out the dough and place
on a cornmeal-dusted pizza peel or
inverted baking sheet, using enough
cornmeal so that the dough slides
easily. Slide the dough onto the
preheated stone and cook until the
bottom begins to crisp, about 3
minutes. Remove the crust from the
oven using a large spatula and place it
uncooked-side down on the peel or
baking sheet, making sure the
underside of the crust is completely
coated with cornmeal. Quickly add the
toppings and slide the pizza back onto
the stone. Continue baking until the
toppings are hot and the bottom of the
crust has browned, 12 to 15 minutes.

Grilled Black Bean Nacho Pizza

Break out the napkins! This pie is an over-the-top vegetarian concoction with black-bean spread, Jack cheese, tomatoes, scallions, olives and pickled jalapeños; it's part nacho, part pizza. This pizza is grilled, which gives it a great flavor and isn't as tricky as it sounds. Just make sure you have all your ingredients ready before you put the dough on the grill. If you prefer to make it in the oven, see Oven Variation.

1 cup canned black beans, rinsed
½ cup chopped jarred roasted red peppers
1 medium clove garlic, quartered
1 tablespoon chili powder
¼ teaspoon salt
  Yellow cornmeal for dusting
1 pound Easy Whole-Wheat Pizza Dough (*page 191*) *or* other prepared whole-wheat dough (*see Note, page 199*)
1 cup shredded Monterey Jack cheese
2 medium plum tomatoes, diced
4 medium scallions, thinly sliced
¼ cup chopped pitted ripe black olives
2 tablespoons chopped pickled jalapeños

1. Preheat grill to low. (*For an oven variation, see left.*)

2. Place beans, peppers, garlic, chili powder and salt in a food processor and process until smooth, scraping down the sides as needed.

3. Sprinkle cornmeal onto a pizza peel or the bottom of a large baking sheet. Roll out or stretch dough on a lightly floured surface into a 14-inch circle. Transfer to the prepared peel or baking sheet, making sure the underside of the dough is completely coated with cornmeal.

4. Slide the crust onto the grill rack; close the lid. Cook until lightly browned, 3 to 4 minutes.

5. Using a large spatula, flip the crust. Spread the bean mixture on the crust, leaving a 1-inch border. Quickly layer on cheese, tomatoes, scallions, olives and pickled jalapeños.

6. Close the lid again and grill until the cheese has melted and the bottom of the crust has browned, about 8 minutes.

MAKES 6 SERVINGS.

Turkish Pasta with Bison Sauce

Who says budget can't be sophisticated? Sweet aromatic spices, cilantro, mint and lemon marry well with ground bison in this delicious pasta sauce. Lean ground beef or turkey would also work well.

2	tablespoons extra-virgin olive oil
1 ½	cups finely chopped onion
1	cup finely chopped carrot
½	cup finely chopped celery
1	tablespoon minced garlic
2	tablespoons paprika
1	teaspoon ground coriander
1	teaspoon kosher salt
1	teaspoon freshly ground pepper, plus more to taste
½	teaspoon ground cumin
¼	teaspoon ground cinnamon
1	pound ground bison (*see Notes*)
½	cup pomegranate juice
1	14-ounce can diced tomatoes
1	cup chopped fresh cilantro, divided
1	tablespoon chopped fresh mint
1	tablespoon lemon juice, plus more to taste
1	pound whole-wheat wide pasta, such as pappardelle *or* fettuccine
½	cup nonfat plain yogurt, preferably Greek-style (*see Notes*)

1. Put a pot of water on to boil.

2. Heat oil in a large, high-sided skillet or Dutch oven over medium heat. Add onion, carrot and celery; cook, covered, stirring occasionally, until softened, about 10 minutes. Add garlic and cook, stirring, for 1 minute more. Stir in paprika, coriander, salt, pepper, cumin and cinnamon. Cook, stirring, until the vegetables are well coated and the spices are fragrant, about 45 seconds.

3. Increase the heat to medium-high and add bison. Cook, stirring and breaking it up with a wooden spoon, until no longer pink, 4 to 6 minutes. Add pomegranate juice and scrape up any browned bits. Stir in tomatoes and their juice, ¾ cup cilantro, mint and 1 tablespoon lemon juice. Bring to a simmer. Reduce heat; cook, uncovered, maintaining a gentle simmer and stirring occasionally, for 15 minutes. Add a little water if the sauce gets too thick; if it's too thin, increase the heat and boil for a few minutes. Season with more pepper and lemon juice, if desired.

4. Meanwhile, cook pasta in boiling water until just tender, about 9 minutes or according to package directions. Drain and divide among 8 shallow bowls. Spoon the sauce over the pasta and garnish with a dollop of yogurt and a sprinkle of the remaining cilantro.

MAKES 8 SERVINGS.

ACTIVE TIME: 1 hour

TOTAL: 1 hour

TO MAKE AHEAD: Cover and refrigerate the sauce (Steps 2-3) for up to 3 days. Reheat on low; thin the sauce with a little water if desired.

PER SERVING:

380 calories; 10 g fat (3 g sat, 3 g mono); 30 mg cholesterol; 54 g carbohydrate; 23 g protein; 10 g fiber; 280 mg sodium; 401 mg potassium.

NUTRITION BONUS:

Vitamin A (80% daily value), Zinc (27% dv), Iron (24% dv), Magnesium (23% dv), Vitamin C (15% dv).

H✕W   H↑F   H♥H

NOTES:

Look for **ground bison** (also called buffalo) at well-stocked supermarkets. Lean ground beef or turkey will also work in this recipe.

Greek-style yogurt is made by removing the whey from cultured milk, which gives the yogurt an extra-thick and creamy texture. Look for it with other yogurt in large supermarkets. You can strain regular yogurt to make it thick like Greek-style yogurt. Line a sieve with cheesecloth and set it over a bowl. (*Alternatively, place a large coffee filter in the sieve.*) Spoon in 1 cup nonfat plain yogurt and let it drain in the refrigerator until reduced to ¾ cup, about 2 hours.

ACTIVE TIME: 40 minutes

TOTAL: 40 minutes

PER SERVING:

374 calories; 6 g fat (1 g sat, 2 g mono); 55 mg cholesterol; 51 g carbohydrate; 29 g protein; 2 g fiber; 775 mg sodium; 975 mg potassium.

NUTRITION BONUS:

Vitamin A (95% daily value), Vitamin C (55% dv), Potassium (28% dv), Magnesium (23% dv), Iron (21% dv), Folate (20% dv), Zinc (19% dv).

H✖W H♥H

NOTES:

Soba (Japanese buckwheat noodles) and **rice noodles** can be found in the Asian section of most supermarkets.

Shao Hsing (or Shaoxing) is a seasoned rice wine available in the Asian or wine section of some supermarkets and in Asian food markets. Once opened, store in the refrigerator for up to 1 year.

Sherry is a type of fortified wine originally from southern Spain. Don't use the "cooking sherry" sold in many supermarkets—it can be surprisingly high in sodium. Instead, purchase dry or medium sherry that's sold with other fortified wines in your wine or liquor store.

Chile-garlic sauce (also labeled chili-garlic sauce or paste) is a blend of ground chiles, garlic and vinegar. It can be found in the Asian section of large supermarkets and will keep for up to 1 year in the refrigerator.

Pork & Bok Choy Stir-Fry

Stir-fries are, by design, made for using whatever you have on hand so that nothing in your fridge goes to waste. This zippy stir-fry is made with julienned pork tenderloin but you could just as easily use sirloin steak or chicken breast instead. We cut the bok choy into long, thin strips to mimic the long noodles. We chose Japanese soba noodles for this dish because they are made with buckwheat, which gives them a nutty flavor and a boost of fiber. You can also use mild-flavored rice noodles or whole-wheat spaghetti. Serve with sliced cucumbers dressed with rice-wine vinegar.

8	ounces soba *or* rice noodles (*see Notes*)
¾-1	pound pork tenderloin, trimmed
⅓	cup water
¼	cup Shao Hsing rice wine *or* dry sherry (*see Notes*)
2	tablespoons reduced-sodium soy sauce
2	teaspoons cornstarch
1	tablespoon peanut oil or canola oil
1	medium onion, thinly sliced
1	pound bok choy (about 1 medium head), trimmed and cut into long, thin strips
1	tablespoon chopped garlic
1	tablespoon chile-garlic sauce (*see Notes*)

1. Bring a large saucepan of water to a boil. Add noodles and cook according to package directions. Drain, rinse with cold water and set aside.

2. Meanwhile, slice pork into thin rounds; cut each round into matchsticks. Whisk water, rice wine (or sherry), soy sauce and cornstarch in a small bowl.

3. Heat oil in a Dutch oven over medium heat. Add onion and cook, stirring occasionally, until beginning to soften, 2 to 3 minutes. Add bok choy and cook, stirring occasionally, until beginning to soften, about 5 minutes. Add the pork, garlic and chile-garlic sauce; cook, stirring, until the pork is just cooked through, 2 to 3 minutes.

4. Whisk the cornstarch mixture again, add it to the pan and bring to a boil. Cook, stirring, until the sauce has thickened, 2 to 4 minutes. Serve the pork and vegetables over the noodles.

MAKES 4 SERVINGS.

ACTIVE TIME: 35 minutes

TOTAL: 35 minutes

PER SERVING:

433 calories; 13 g fat (5 g sat, 5 g mono); 75 mg cholesterol; 42 g carbohydrate; 34 g protein; 5 g fiber; 491 mg sodium; 483 mg potassium.

NUTRITION BONUS:

Vitamin C (38% daily value), Calcium (37% dv).

H⬆F   H♥H

NOTE:

To poach **chicken breasts**, place boneless, skinless chicken breasts in a medium skillet or saucepan. Figure 4 ounces raw chicken for each 1 cup shredded or diced cooked chicken. Add lightly salted water to cover and bring to a boil. Cover, reduce heat to low and simmer gently until chicken is cooked through and no longer pink in the middle, 10 to 15 minutes.

Cheesy Chicken Pasta

This creamy pasta is a crowd pleaser for adults and kids alike—a sophisticated macaroni-and-cheese of sorts. Here, it's tossed with cooked chicken or turkey and cauliflower, but in a pinch, you could use a couple cans of tuna and broccoli or even peas. Mix and match with what you have on hand. Serve with a spinach salad.

8	ounces whole-wheat penne
2	cups cauliflower florets (½-inch)
1	tablespoon extra-virgin olive oil
½	cup finely chopped onion
½	cup dry white wine
3	cups low-fat milk
3	tablespoons all-purpose flour
¾	teaspoon salt
½	teaspoon freshly ground pepper
1	cup shredded Gruyère *or* Swiss cheese
3	cups shredded cooked chicken *or* turkey (12 ounces; *see Note*)
1	teaspoon Dijon mustard
2	tablespoons chopped fresh chives *or* scallion greens

1. Bring a large pot of water to a boil. Add pasta and cook for 5 minutes. Add cauliflower and cook until the pasta and cauliflower are tender, about 4 minutes more. Drain, rinse and return to the pot.

2. Meanwhile, heat oil in a large saucepan over medium heat. Add onion and cook, stirring, until tender, 2 to 3 minutes. Add wine and cook until reduced slightly, about 1 minute. Whisk milk, flour, salt and pepper together in a medium bowl and add to the pan. Bring to a boil over medium-high heat, stirring frequently. Cook, stirring, until thickened, about 1 minute. Reduce heat to low and stir in cheese until smooth. Stir chicken (or turkey) and mustard into the cheese sauce; cook until heated through, about 2 minutes.

3. Stir the sauce into the drained pasta and cauliflower. Serve sprinkled with chives (or scallion greens).

MAKES 6 SERVINGS, ABOUT 1⅓ CUPS EACH.

Pasta with Broccoli, Tomatoes & Anchovy Sauce

ACTIVE TIME: 40 minutes

TOTAL: 40 minutes

PER SERVING:

176 calories; 5 g fat (1 g sat, 2 g mono); 8 mg cholesterol; 25 g carbohydrate; 10 g protein; 7 g fiber; 430 mg sodium; 382 mg potassium.

NUTRITION BONUS:

Vitamin C (142% daily value), Vitamin A (32% dv), Folate (17% dv).

H✄W   H⬆F   H♥H

Pasta is one of the ultimate value meals and whole-grain pasta makes it healthier and more satisfying. Here, a touch of anchovy makes broccoli and whole-wheat spaghetti sing. For a more pungent variation, use broccoli rabe (also called broccoli raab or rapini) instead of the broccoli. To make it a meal, begin with an arugula salad tossed with lemon vinaigrette.

1½	pounds broccoli
1	tablespoon extra-virgin olive oil
2	cloves garlic, minced
1½	teaspoons anchovy paste
¼	teaspoon crushed red pepper
1	28-ounce can whole tomatoes, chopped, juice reserved
¼	teaspoon salt
¼	teaspoon freshly ground pepper
12	ounces whole-wheat spaghetti *or* linguine
6	tablespoons freshly grated Parmesan cheese

1. Put a pot of water on to boil.

2. Cut broccoli florets from stems and cut them into 1-inch pieces. Peel, halve and slice the stems.

3. Heat oil in a large skillet over medium heat. Add garlic, anchovy paste and crushed red pepper. Cook, stirring constantly, until the garlic is fragrant, about 1 minute. Add the broccoli stems, tomatoes and their juice and bring to a simmer; cook, stirring occasionally, until thickened, 12 to 15 minutes. Add the broccoli florets; cover and cook until tender, 5 to 10 minutes more. Season with salt and pepper.

4. Meanwhile, cook pasta until just tender, 8 to 10 minutes or according to package directions. Drain and transfer to a large bowl; toss with the sauce. Serve immediately, sprinkled with Parmesan.

MAKES 6 SERVINGS, ABOUT 1⅔ CUPS EACH.

ACTIVE TIME: 30 minutes

TOTAL: 30 minutes

PER SERVING:

402 calories; 12 g fat (3 g sat, 6 g mono); 7 mg cholesterol; 62 g carbohydrate; 12 g protein; 9 g fiber; 546 mg sodium; 738 mg potassium.

NUTRITION BONUS:

Vitamin C (143% daily value), Vitamin A (116% dv), Potassium (21% dv), Iron (15% dv).

H↑F   H♥H

Sweet Potato & Red Pepper Pasta

The sweet potato is a great nutritional value. It's loaded with beta carotene, which helps keep your eyes healthy. In this colorful pasta recipe it is paired with another "power vegetable," red bell pepper, which is loaded with vitamin C, along with diced plum tomatoes and creamy goat cheese. The dish is bursting with parsley and tarragon, but any fresh herbs you have on hand, such as basil, oregano or chives, will do. Serve with a garden salad.

8	ounces whole-wheat angel hair pasta
2	tablespoons extra-virgin olive oil, divided
4	cloves garlic, minced
3	cups shredded, peeled sweet potato (about 1 medium)
1	large red bell pepper, thinly sliced
1	cup diced plum tomatoes
½	cup water
2	tablespoons chopped fresh parsley
1	tablespoon chopped fresh tarragon
1	tablespoon white-wine vinegar *or* lemon juice
¾	teaspoon salt
½	cup crumbled goat cheese

1. Bring a large pot of water to a boil. Cook pasta until just tender, 4 to 5 minutes or according to package directions.

2. Meanwhile, place 1 tablespoon oil and garlic in a large skillet. Cook over medium heat, stirring occasionally, until the garlic is sizzling and fragrant, 2 to 5 minutes. Add sweet potato, bell pepper, tomatoes and water and cook, stirring occasionally, until the bell pepper is tender-crisp, 5 to 7 minutes. Remove from the heat; cover and keep warm.

3. Drain the pasta, reserving ½ cup of the cooking water. Return the pasta to the pot. Add the vegetable mixture, the remaining 1 tablespoon oil, parsley, tarragon, vinegar (or lemon juice), salt and cheese; toss to combine. Add the reserved pasta water, 2 tablespoons at a time, to achieve the desired consistency.

MAKES 4 SERVINGS, ABOUT 1 ³/₄ CUPS EACH.

Zucchini, Fennel & White Bean Pasta

Beans have been called the poor man's meat because they are an inexpensive and filling source of protein. In this recipe, along with roasted vegetables, fresh mint and tangy, salty aged goat cheese, beans transform a humble pasta into a soul-satisfying gourmet dish. When making a pasta dish with beans, you can use some of the bean-cooking liquid to give the sauce silky body and help it cling to the pasta. If you're using canned beans, use some of the pasta-cooking liquid or just water.

1	large fennel bulb, trimmed
2	medium zucchini
3	tablespoons extra-virgin olive oil, divided
¼	teaspoon salt
8	ounces whole-wheat penne *or* similar short pasta
2	cloves garlic, finely chopped
1	cup cooked cannellini beans (*see How to Cook Beans, page 191*) *or* rinsed canned beans
½	cup bean-cooking liquid, pasta-cooking liquid *or* water
2	plum tomatoes, diced
¾	cup crumbled hard, aged goat cheese *or* fresh goat cheese
¼	cup chopped fresh mint leaves
	Freshly ground pepper to taste

1. Preheat oven to 400°F.

2. Cut fennel bulb in half lengthwise and then slice lengthwise into ½-inch-thick wedges. Quarter zucchini lengthwise. Toss the fennel and zucchini with 1 tablespoon oil and salt. Arrange in a single layer on a large baking sheet. Roast, turning once, until soft and beginning to brown, about 20 minutes.

3. Meanwhile, bring a large pot of water to a boil. Add pasta; cook until just tender, 8 to 10 minutes or according to package directions.

4. Heat the remaining 2 tablespoons oil in a large skillet over medium heat. Add garlic and cook, stirring, for 30 seconds. Remove from the heat.

5. When the vegetables are cool enough to handle, coarsely chop. Add the vegetables, beans and bean-cooking liquid (or other liquid) to the pan with the garlic and place over medium-low heat. Drain the pasta and immediately add it to the pan. Toss thoroughly and add tomatoes; toss until just warm. Remove from the heat and stir in cheese and mint. Season with pepper.

MAKES 4 SERVINGS, ABOUT 2¼ CUPS EACH.

ACTIVE TIME: 40 minutes

TOTAL: 40 minutes

PER SERVING:

515 calories; 22 g fat (7 g sat, 11 g mono); 22 mg cholesterol; 63 g carbohydrate; 20 g protein; 12 g fiber; 350 mg sodium; 990 mg potassium.

NUTRITION BONUS:

Vitamin C (50% daily value), Calcium, Folate & Potassium (28% dv), Iron (26% dv), Vitamin A (25% dv), Magnesium (16% dv).

H ⬆ F

··· SAVE ···························

Adding beans to pasta, soups or salads is a healthy, inexpensive way to add protein and stretch the number of servings. Buying beans dry and in bulk is the most cost-effective way to go, but canned are supremely convenient and still a great value. Turn to page 191 for how to cook beans on the stove or in a slow cooker.

ACTIVE TIME: 25 minutes

TOTAL: 35 minutes

PER SERVING:

258 calories; 8 g fat (2 g sat, 4 g mono); 146 mg cholesterol; 35 g carbohydrate; 13 g protein; 6 g fiber; 523 mg sodium; 256 mg potassium.

H✱W   H⬆F   H♥H

Spaghetti Frittata

Here's a creative way to use leftover cooked spaghetti: try mixing it with eggs for a filling Italian omelet. If you don't want to buy separate bunches of fresh herbs, look for an Italian blend package that may contain some of each or use one-third the amount of dried.

8	ounces uncooked whole-wheat spaghetti *or* 4 cups cooked
4	teaspoons extra-virgin olive oil
3	medium onions, chopped
4	large eggs
½	cup nonfat milk
⅓	cup freshly grated Parmesan cheese
2	tablespoons chopped fresh parsley
2	tablespoons chopped fresh basil
1	teaspoon salt
½	teaspoon freshly ground pepper
1	tomato, diced (optional)

1. Preheat oven to 450°F.

2. Put a large pot of water on to boil. (Skip this step if using leftover spaghetti.) Cook spaghetti until just tender, 8 to 10 minutes or according to package directions. Drain and refresh with cold water.

3. Meanwhile, heat oil in a large ovenproof nonstick skillet over medium heat. Add onions and cook, stirring occasionally, until golden, 10 to 12 minutes. Transfer the onions to a bowl and let cool slightly. Wipe out the pan.

4. Whisk eggs and milk in a large bowl. Stir in the onions, Parmesan, parsley, basil, salt and pepper. Add the spaghetti.

5. Coat the pan well with cooking spray and heat over medium heat. Pour in the egg mixture and distribute evenly in the pan. Cook until the underside is golden, turning the pan around on the burner occasionally to ensure even cooking, 3 to 5 minutes.

6. Transfer the pan to the oven and bake until the frittata is set in the middle, 10 to 12 minutes. Garnish with tomato, if using.

MAKES 6 SERVINGS.

Mediterranean Tuna Panini

Canned fish, especially salmon, tuna and sardines, are a convenient way to enjoy the health benefits of seafood for less than the cost of fresh. For this filling sandwich, canned tuna is spiked with salty olives and capers, bright lemon juice and tangy feta.

ACTIVE TIME: 25 minutes

TOTAL: 25 minutes

PER SERVING:

287 calories; 7 g fat (2 g sat, 3 g mono); 21 mg cholesterol; 34 g carbohydrate; 20 g protein; 4 g fiber; 566 mg sodium; 149 mg potassium.

NUTRITION BONUS:

Iron (16% daily value).

H✶W   H♥H

2   5- to 6-ounce cans water-packed chunk light tuna, drained
1   plum tomato, chopped
¼   cup crumbled feta cheese
2   tablespoons chopped marinated artichoke hearts
2   tablespoons minced red onion
1   tablespoon chopped pitted kalamata olives
1   teaspoon capers, rinsed and chopped
1   teaspoon lemon juice
    Freshly ground pepper to taste
8   slices whole-wheat bread
2   teaspoons canola oil

1. Have four 15-ounce cans and a medium skillet (not nonstick) ready by the stove.

2. Place tuna in a medium bowl and flake with a fork. Add tomato, feta, artichoke hearts, onion, olives, capers, lemon juice and pepper; stir to combine. Divide the tuna mixture among 4 slices of bread (about ½ cup each). Top with the remaining bread.

3. Heat 1 teaspoon oil in a large nonstick skillet over medium heat. Place 2 sandwiches in the pan. Place the medium skillet on top of the sandwiches, then place the cans in the skillet to weight it down. Cook the sandwiches until golden on one side, about 2 minutes. Reduce the heat to medium-low, flip the sandwiches, replace the top skillet and cans, and cook until the second side is golden, 1 to 3 minutes more. Repeat with another 1 teaspoon oil and the remaining sandwiches.

MAKES 4 SERVINGS.

⋯SAVE⋯

Love panini (those crispy grill-pressed sandwiches) but don't want to buy a panini maker? No problem. You can improvise and get the same effect with two skillets and four 15-ounce cans of beans, soup or whatever. (*See recipe, left.*) Try other combinations of fillings for panini, such as turkey, Swiss, avocado and onion or ham, honey mustard, Cheddar and arugula.

ACTIVE TIME: 25 minutes

TOTAL: 25 minutes

PER SERVING:

209 calories; 3 g fat (0 g sat, 1 g mono); 0 mg cholesterol; 37 g carbohydrate; 10 g protein; 9 g fiber; 696 mg sodium; 781 mg potassium.

NUTRITION BONUS:

Potassium (22% daily value), Folate (20% dv), Magnesium & Vitamin C (18% dv).

H✕W H⬆F H♥H

NOTE:

The dark gills found on the underside of a **portobello mushroom cap** are edible, but can turn a dish an unappealing gray/black color. Gently scrape the gills off with a spoon.

Grilled Eggplant & Portobello Sandwich

If the price of high-quality meat is getting you down and you're searching for a vegetarian option for your next cookout, look no further. Grilled eggplant and portobello mushrooms have meaty texture and delicious, smoky flavor that make them perfect stand-ins for ground beef or steak in a sandwich. For extra flavor, we top it with slices of garden-fresh tomato and spicy arugula. Serve with a mixed green salad.

1	small clove garlic, chopped
1/4	cup low-fat mayonnaise
1	teaspoon lemon juice
1	medium eggplant (about 1 pound), sliced into 1/2-inch rounds
2	large *or* 3 medium portobello mushroom caps, gills removed if desired (*see Note*)
	Canola *or* olive oil cooking spray
1/2	teaspoon salt
1/2	teaspoon freshly ground pepper
8	slices whole-wheat sandwich bread, lightly grilled *or* toasted
2	cups arugula *or* spinach, stemmed and chopped if large
1	large tomato, sliced

1. Preheat grill to medium-high.

2. Mash garlic into a paste on a cutting board with the back of a spoon. Combine with mayonnaise and lemon juice in a small bowl. Set aside.

3. Coat both sides of eggplant rounds and mushroom caps with cooking spray and season with salt and pepper. Grill the vegetables, turning once, until tender and browned on both sides, 2 to 4 minutes per side. When cool enough to handle, slice the mushrooms.

4. Spread 1½ teaspoons of the garlic mayonnaise on each piece of bread. Layer the eggplant, mushrooms, arugula (or spinach) and tomato slices onto 4 slices of bread and top with the remaining bread.

MAKES 4 SERVINGS.

ACTIVE TIME: 20 minutes

TOTAL: 20 minutes

PER SERVING:

264 calories; 8 g fat (3 g sat, 4 g mono); 10 mg cholesterol; 39 g carbohydrate; 14 g protein; 8 g fiber; 624 mg sodium; 174 mg potassium.

NUTRITION BONUS:

Vitamin C (20% daily value), Vitamin A (15% dv).

H✖W   H⬆F   H❤H

····· SAVE ·····

Be flexible and ready to improvise when you cook so that you can use up what you have on hand rather than following every ingredient to a T. For example, you could try this recipe with Cheddar instead of provolone, red-wine vinegar instead of balsamic or jarred roasted red peppers instead of artichoke hearts. The flavor might be a little different, but you may discover a combo you love!

Italian Vegetable Hoagies

Having a sandwich for a light lunch or dinner is easy on the waistline as well as the wallet. This delightfully easy, and somewhat messy, hoagie packs a punch with sweet balsamic vinegar, artichoke hearts, red onion, provolone cheese and zesty pepperoncini. Serve with tomato-and-cucumber salad.

¼ cup thinly sliced red onion, separated into rings
1   14-ounce can artichoke hearts, rinsed and coarsely chopped
1   medium tomato, seeded and diced
2   tablespoons balsamic vinegar
1   tablespoon extra-virgin olive oil
1   teaspoon dried oregano
1   16- to 20-inch-long baguette, preferably whole-grain
2   slices provolone cheese (about 2 ounces), halved
2   cups shredded romaine lettuce
¼ cup sliced pepperoncini (optional)

1. Place onion rings in a small bowl and add cold water to cover. Set aside while you prepare the remaining ingredients.

2. Combine artichoke hearts, tomato, vinegar, oil and oregano in a medium bowl. Cut baguette into 4 equal lengths. Split each piece horizontally and pull out about half of the soft bread from each side. (Save the insides of the bread in an airtight container to make breadcrumbs. *See page 198.*) Drain the onions and pat dry.

3. To assemble sandwiches, divide provolone among the bottom pieces of baguette. Spread on the artichoke mixture and top with the onion, lettuce and pepperoncini, if using. Cover with the baguette tops. Serve immediately.

MAKES 4 SERVINGS.

Tijuana Torta

A good selection of canned beans is a must-have pantry staple for the cost-conscious healthy cook. They are packed with protein, fiber and minerals, plus they're available in enough varieties to make a world traveler's head spin. Here, they are paired with a fresh, quick guacamole in a Mexican-style torta, which is just like a burrito, except the "wrapper" is a hollowed-out roll instead of a tortilla. Take this vegetarian version to another level (and add calcium) by melting Monterey Jack cheese onto the bean side of the sandwich. Serve with corn on the cob or a mixed green salad.

1	15-ounce can black beans *or* pinto beans, rinsed (*see Note*), *or* 1 ½ cups cooked (*see How to Cook Beans, page 191*)
3	tablespoons prepared salsa
1	tablespoon chopped pickled jalapeño
½	teaspoon ground cumin
1	ripe avocado, pitted
2	tablespoons minced onion
1	tablespoon lime juice
1	16- to 20-inch-long baguette, preferably whole-grain
1 ⅓	cups shredded green cabbage

1. Mash beans, salsa, jalapeño and cumin in a small bowl. Mash avocado, onion and lime juice in another small bowl.

2. Cut baguette into 4 equal lengths. Split each piece in half horizontally. Pull out most of the soft bread from the center so you're left with mostly crust. (Save the insides of the bread in an airtight container to make breadcrumbs. *See page 198.*) Divide the bean paste, avocado mixture and cabbage evenly among the sandwiches. Cut each sandwich in half and serve.

MAKES 4 SERVINGS.

ACTIVE TIME: 25 minutes

TOTAL: 25 minutes

TO MAKE AHEAD: Cover and refrigerate the bean mixture (Step 1) for up to 3 days.

PER SERVING:

354 calories; 9 g fat (1 g sat, 5 g mono); 0 mg cholesterol; 60 g carbohydrate; 17 g protein; 17 g fiber; 822 mg sodium; 639 mg potassium.

NUTRITION BONUS:

Folate & Vitamin C (29% daily value), Potassium (18% dv).

H✂W   H⬆F   H♥H

NOTE:

Canned beans are convenient but tend to be high in sodium. Give them a good rinse before adding to a recipe to rid them of some of their sodium (up to 35 percent) or opt for low-sodium or no-salt-added varieties. Or, if you have the time, cook your own beans from scratch. You'll find recipes for cooking beans on the stovetop or in a slow cooker on page 191.

ACTIVE TIME: 30 minutes

TOTAL: 30 minutes

PER SERVING:

353 calories; 15 g fat (5 g sat, 6 g mono); 79 mg cholesterol; 25 g carbohydrate; 29 g protein; 4 g fiber; 612 mg sodium; 522 mg potassium.

NUTRITION BONUS:

Calcium (19% daily value), Magnesium (16% dv), Potassium (15% dv).

Stuffed Pork Sandwich

The classic Cuban sandwich inspired this recipe. The original is made with ham, roasted pork, Swiss cheese and pickles pressed and griddled between two pieces of soft white bread. Our version cuts down on the meat and is served on a soft whole-wheat bun. Serve with vinegary coleslaw.

4	4-ounce boneless pork chops, 1/2 inch thick, trimmed
2	thin slices Swiss cheese (1 ounce each), cut in half
4	dill pickle sandwich slices
1/4	teaspoon salt
1/4	teaspoon freshly ground pepper
1	tablespoon canola oil
4	whole-wheat hamburger buns, toasted
2	teaspoons Dijon mustard
4	slices tomato
2	romaine lettuce leaves, cut in half

1. Cut each pork chop nearly in half horizontally, stopping short of the opposite side. Open each chop and place between sheets of plastic wrap. Pound with a meat mallet or heavy skillet until flattened to an even thickness, slightly thicker than 1/8 inch.

2. Place a piece of cheese and a pickle slice on one side of each flattened chop. Fold the chop over the filling, closing it like a book. Press the edges firmly together to seal. Season both sides with salt and pepper.

3. Heat oil in a large skillet over medium-high heat. Add the stuffed chops, reduce heat to medium and cook until golden brown and cooked through, 3 to 5 minutes per side.

4. To assemble sandwiches, spread the toasted buns with mustard and top each with a pork chop, tomato slice and lettuce.

MAKES 4 SERVINGS.

3 VEGETARIAN

Going meatless a few times a week is good for your health (you'll be eating less saturated fat), good for your wallet (meat is often the most expensive food on the plate) and good for the environment. You can eat vegetarian and still be satisfied, by including ingredients like rice, eggs, beans and tofu.

Sweet Potato & Tofu Red Curry (*page 68*)

ACTIVE TIME: 40 minutes

TOTAL: 40 minutes

PER SERVING:

313 calories; 16 g fat (6 g sat, 4 g mono); 0 mg cholesterol; 34 g carbohydrate; 13 g protein; 7 g fiber; 473 mg sodium; 665 mg potassium.

NUTRITION BONUS:

Vitamin A (120% daily value), Vitamin C (45% dv), Calcium (24% dv), Potassium (19% dv), Iron (15% dv).

H↑F

Sweet Potato & Tofu Red Curry

You can skip all the separate spices and other seasonings because red Thai curry paste is a convenient blend of chile peppers, garlic, lemongrass and galangal (a root that's similar in flavor to ginger) that will add a multitude of flavors to a dish from just one jar. It can pack a lot of heat, so be sure to taste as you go. Look for the curry paste in jars or cans in the Asian section of the supermarket or specialty store. Leftover curry paste can be kept in the freezer for up to a year. Ladle the stew over rice to soak up every bit of the delicious sauce. (Photograph: page 66.)

1	14-ounce package extra-firm tofu, drained
4	teaspoons canola oil, divided
1	pound sweet potato, scrubbed and cut into 1-inch cubes
1	14-ounce can "lite" coconut milk
½	cup vegetable broth *or* reduced-sodium chicken broth
1-2	teaspoons red Thai curry paste
8	ounces green beans, trimmed and cut into 1-inch pieces
1	tablespoon brown sugar
2	teaspoons lime juice
½	teaspoon salt
⅓	cup chopped fresh cilantro
1	lime, quartered

1. Cut tofu into 1-inch cubes and pat dry. Heat 2 teaspoons oil in a large nonstick skillet over medium-high heat. Add tofu and cook, stirring every 2 or 3 minutes, until browned, 6 to 8 minutes total. Transfer to a plate.

2. Heat the remaining 2 teaspoons oil over medium-high heat. Add sweet potato and cook, stirring occasionally, until browned, 4 to 5 minutes. Add coconut milk, broth and curry paste to taste. Bring to a boil; reduce to a simmer and cook, covered, stirring occasionally, until the sweet potato is just tender, about 4 minutes. Add the tofu, green beans and brown sugar; return to a simmer and cook, covered, stirring occasionally, until the green beans are tender-crisp, 2 to 4 minutes. Stir in lime juice and salt. Sprinkle with cilantro and serve with lime wedges.

MAKES 4 SERVINGS, ABOUT 1 ½ CUPS EACH.

Szechuan Tofu & Green Bean Stir-Fry

This spicy stir-fry is a great way to use green beans when they're bountiful and inexpensive at the supermarket. You can also try it with other vegetables, such as broccoli or peppers, just make sure to cut them into small pieces so that they cook quickly. Coating the tofu in cornstarch before you cook it gives it a great texture on the outside. (Photograph: page 12.)

½	cup water, divided
¼	cup reduced-sodium soy sauce
1	tablespoon tomato paste
2	teaspoons Chinkiang vinegar (*see Note*) *or* balsamic vinegar
2	teaspoons sugar
¼-½	teaspoon crushed red pepper, or to taste
1	teaspoon plus 2 tablespoons cornstarch, divided
1	14-ounce package extra-firm tofu, drained
2	tablespoons canola oil, divided
4	cups green beans, trimmed and cut in half
4	cloves garlic, minced
2	teaspoons minced fresh ginger

1. Whisk ¼ cup water, soy sauce, tomato paste, vinegar, sugar, crushed red pepper to taste and 1 teaspoon cornstarch in a small bowl. Set aside. Cut tofu into ½- to ¾-inch cubes and pat dry. Toss the tofu in a bowl with the remaining 2 tablespoons cornstarch to coat.

2. Heat 1 tablespoon oil in a wok or large skillet over medium-high heat. Add the tofu and spread out across the surface of the pan. Let cook undisturbed for 2 minutes. Gently turn and stir. Continue cooking, stirring occasionally, until lightly browned and crispy, 2 to 3 minutes more. Transfer to a plate.

3. Reduce heat to medium. Add the remaining 1 tablespoon oil to the pan. Add green beans, garlic and ginger and cook, stirring constantly, for 1 minute. Add the remaining ¼ cup water, cover and cook until the beans are crisp-tender, 2 to 4 minutes. Stir the reserved soy sauce mixture and pour it over the green beans. Cook, stirring, until thickened, about 1 minute. Add the tofu and cook, stirring, until heated through, about 1 minute more.

MAKES 4 SERVINGS, 1 ½ CUPS EACH.

ACTIVE TIME: 30 minutes

TOTAL: 30 minutes

PER SERVING:

249 calories; 12 g fat (1 g sat, 4 g mono); 0 mg cholesterol; 21 g carbohydrate; 14 g protein; 5 g fiber; 661 mg sodium; 217 mg potassium.

NUTRITION BONUS:

Vitamin C (21% daily value), Vitamin A (17% dv).

NOTE:

Chinkiang is a dark, slightly sweet vinegar with a smoky flavor. It is available in many Asian specialty markets. If unavailable, balsamic vinegar is an acceptable substitute.

···SAVE···········

Ever open a can of tomato paste just to use 1 or 2 tablespoons in a recipe? Try freezing the leftovers in little blocks in an ice cube tray, then store them in a sealable plastic bag in the freezer until you're ready to use them. Or look for tomato paste in a tube, which can be kept for months in the refrigerator after it's opened.

ACTIVE TIME: 25 minutes

TOTAL: 40 minutes

PER SERVING:

202 calories; 12 g fat (2 g sat, 6 g mono); 0 mg cholesterol; 13 g carbohydrate; 13 g protein; 5 g fiber; 643 mg sodium; 421 mg potassium.

NUTRITION BONUS:

Folate (36% daily value), Vitamin C (30% dv), Calcium (29% dv), Vitamin A (19% dv), Iron (17% dv), Magnesium (16% dv).

H✳W   H⬆F   H♥H

NOTE:

Red miso (akamiso) is a salty fermented paste made from barley or rice and soybeans. Find it in the refrigerated section near tofu. Use it for sauces, marinades or soup. Store in the refrigerator for up to 1 year.

Savory Orange-Roasted Tofu & Asparagus

If you've never had roasted tofu before, here's a great way to start. Toss tofu and asparagus in a tangy orange- and basil-scented sauce, made rich and savory with miso. While miso can be a bit pricy, it is an excellent ingredient to add to marinades, dressings and sauces, and once opened, it keeps for a year or more in the refrigerator. Serve this dish with brown rice or couscous and an orange-and-fennel salad.

1   14-ounce package extra-firm water-packed tofu, drained
2   tablespoons red miso (*see Note*), divided
2   tablespoons balsamic vinegar, divided
4   teaspoons extra-virgin olive oil, divided
1   pound asparagus, trimmed and cut into 1-inch pieces
3   tablespoons chopped fresh basil
1   teaspoon freshly grated orange zest
¼   cup orange juice
¼   teaspoon salt

1. Preheat oven to 450°F. Coat a large baking sheet with cooking spray.

2. Cut tofu into ½-inch cubes and pat dry. Whisk 1 tablespoon miso, 1 tablespoon vinegar and 2 teaspoons oil in a large bowl until smooth. Add the tofu; gently toss to coat. Spread the tofu in an even layer on the prepared baking sheet. Roast for 15 minutes. Gently toss asparagus with the tofu. Return to the oven and roast until the tofu is golden brown and the asparagus is tender, 8 to 10 minutes more.

3. Meanwhile, whisk the remaining 1 tablespoon miso, 1 tablespoon vinegar, 2 teaspoons oil, basil, orange zest, orange juice and salt in the large bowl until smooth. Toss the roasted tofu and asparagus with the sauce and serve.

MAKES 3 SERVINGS, 1 ¼ CUPS EACH.

ACTIVE TIME: 40 minutes

TOTAL: 40 minutes

PER SERVING:

366 calories; 14 g fat (2 g sat, 6 g mono); 212 g cholesterol; 46 g carbohydrate; 14 g protein; 5 g fiber; 581 mg sodium; 453 mg potassium.

NUTRITION BONUS:

Vitamin C (140% daily value), Vitamin A (70% dv), Folate (24% dv), Magnesium (22% dv), Iron (18% dv).

H↑F   H♥H

Vegetable Fried Rice

Fried rice was created for using up leftover rice and vegetables. We've made this light and easy version with instant brown rice, but if you have leftover cold rice, use that instead and skip Step 1. Asparagus, bell pepper and scallions are a nice blend, especially for springtime, but you could really use any vegetables you have on hand and still get tasty results. (Photograph: page 12.)

1   cup instant brown rice
1   cup vegetable broth
2   large eggs, lightly beaten
2   teaspoons canola oil
6   ounces asparagus spears, trimmed and cut into 1-inch pieces (about ½ bunch)
1   medium red bell pepper, thinly sliced into 1-inch pieces
4   scallions, cut into 1-inch pieces
1   clove garlic, minced
1   tablespoon minced fresh ginger
4   teaspoons reduced-sodium soy sauce
2   tablespoons rice vinegar
1   teaspoon toasted sesame oil
    Hot red pepper sauce to taste

1. Combine rice and broth in a small saucepan. Bring to a boil over high heat. Cover, reduce heat and simmer until the liquid is absorbed, 12 to 14 minutes. Spread the rice out on a large plate and let stand for 5 minutes.

2. While the rice is cooling, coat a large nonstick wok or skillet with cooking spray and place over medium heat. Pour in eggs and cook, stirring gently, until just set, 30 seconds to 1 minute. Transfer to a small bowl.

3. Heat canola oil in the pan over medium-high; add asparagus and cook, stirring, for 2 minutes. Add bell pepper, scallions, garlic and ginger; cook, stirring, until the vegetables are just tender, about 2 minutes. Add the cooked rice, soy sauce and vinegar to the pan; cook until the liquid is absorbed, 30 seconds to 1 minute. Fold in the cooked eggs. Remove from the heat; stir in sesame oil and hot sauce.

MAKES 2 SERVINGS, 2 CUPS EACH.

Okra & Chickpea Tagine

This quick and easy stew made with fresh or frozen okra and canned chickpeas is packed with Moroccan flavors. The name "tagine" refers to the two-part, cone-shaped casserole dish in which countless slow-cooked Moroccan dishes are prepared. You don't need to prepare this in a tagine dish—it works well in a large saucepan—but if you have one, here's a chance to use it. If you can get your hands on canned fava beans, they make an excellent substitute for the chickpeas. Serve over rice or couscous.

1	pound fresh *or* frozen okra, stem ends trimmed, cut into ½-inch pieces
10	sprigs fresh cilantro, plus more leaves for garnish
2	tablespoons extra-virgin olive oil
1	red bell pepper, finely diced
1	medium onion, finely diced
3	cloves garlic, minced
½	teaspoon ground ginger
½	teaspoon freshly ground pepper
3	plum tomatoes, diced, *or* 1 cup drained canned diced tomatoes
½	cup vegetable broth *or* reduced-sodium chicken broth
¾	teaspoon ground cumin
1	15-ounce can chickpeas, rinsed, *or* 1 ⅓ cups cooked (*see How to Cook Beans, page 191*)
¾	teaspoon salt
1	teaspoon harissa (*see Note*) *or* hot sauce, or to taste

1. Place a large bowl of ice water next to the stove. Bring a large saucepan of water to a boil. Add okra and cook for 2 minutes. Transfer the okra with a slotted spoon to the ice water. Drain.

2. Tie cilantro sprigs together with kitchen string.

3. Heat oil in a tagine dish set over a heat diffuser or a large saucepan over medium-high heat. Add bell pepper. Cook, stirring, until soft, 2 to 5 minutes. Transfer to a bowl with a slotted spoon.

4. Add onion, garlic, ginger and pepper to the pan. Cook, stirring, until the onion is soft, 3 to 6 minutes. Mix in tomatoes, broth, cumin, the okra, cilantro sprigs and half the bell pepper. Reduce heat to medium; partially cover. Cook, stirring occasionally, until the okra is soft, 10 to 15 minutes. Stir in chickpeas and salt; cook for 4 minutes. Remove from the heat; discard the cilantro sprigs. Stir in harissa (or hot sauce). Serve sprinkled with the remaining bell pepper and cilantro leaves, if desired.

MAKES 4 SERVINGS, 1 ¼ CUPS EACH.

ACTIVE TIME: 50 minutes

TOTAL: 50 minutes

EQUIPMENT: Kitchen string

PER SERVING:

204 calories; 9 g fat (1 g sat, 5 g mono); 0 mg cholesterol; 30 g carbohydrate; 8 g protein; 11 g fiber; 665 mg sodium; 583 mg potassium.

NUTRITION BONUS:

Vitamin C (120% daily value), Vitamin A (38% dv), Folate (30% dv), Magnesium (19% dv).

H�֍W   H⬆F   H♥H

NOTE:

Harissa is a fiery Tunisian chile paste commonly used in North African cooking. Find it at specialty-food stores, *mustaphas.com* or *amazon.com*. Harissa in a tube will be much hotter than that in a jar. You can substitute Chinese or Thai chile-garlic sauce for it. Try blending leftover harissa with mayonnaise for a spicy sandwich spread or stir it into hummus to give it a kick.

Cheese-&-Spinach-Stuffed Portobellos

Here we take the elements of a vegetarian lasagna filling—ricotta, spinach and Parmesan cheese—and nestle them into roasted portobello mushroom caps. Look for large portobello caps in the bins of loose mushrooms that most supermarkets have. They'll be cheaper than packaged, plus you can pick out the best quality and only buy as many as you need. If you can only find smaller ones, buy one or two extra and divide the filling among all the caps. Serve with a tossed salad and whole-wheat dinner rolls or spaghetti tossed with marinara sauce.

ACTIVE TIME: 20 minutes

TOTAL: 40 minutes

PER SERVING:

201 calories; 10 g fat (5 g sat, 4 g mono); 28 mg cholesterol; 13 g carbohydrate; 14 g protein; 2 g fiber; 680 mg sodium; 677 mg potassium.

NUTRITION BONUS:

Calcium (31% daily value), Vitamin A (25% dv), Potassium (19% dv).

H✳W

- 4 large portobello mushroom caps
- ¼ teaspoon salt
- ¼ teaspoon freshly ground pepper, divided
- 1 cup part-skim ricotta cheese
- 1 cup finely chopped fresh spinach
- ½ cup finely shredded Parmesan cheese, divided
- 2 tablespoons finely chopped kalamata olives
- ½ teaspoon Italian seasoning
- ¾ cup prepared marinara sauce

1. Preheat oven to 450°F. Coat a rimmed baking sheet with cooking spray.

2. Place mushroom caps, gill-side up, on the prepared pan. Sprinkle with salt and ⅛ teaspoon pepper. Roast until tender, 20 to 25 minutes.

3. Meanwhile, mash ricotta, spinach, ¼ cup Parmesan, olives, Italian seasoning and the remaining ⅛ teaspoon pepper in a medium bowl. Place marinara sauce in a small bowl, cover and microwave on High until hot, 30 seconds to 1½ minutes.

4. When the mushrooms are tender, carefully pour out any liquid accumulated in the caps. Return the caps to the pan gill-side up. Spread 1 tablespoon marinara into each cap; cover the remaining sauce to keep warm. Mound a generous ⅓ cup ricotta filling into each cap and sprinkle with the remaining ¼ cup Parmesan. Bake until hot, about 10 minutes. Serve with the remaining marinara sauce.

MAKES 4 SERVINGS.

SAVE

Dollop leftover ricotta cheese on top of your favorite pasta dinner, such as Spaghetti Frittata (*page 56*), or use it in place of the goat cheese in Sweet Potato & Red Pepper Pasta (*page 52*). Or mix it with melted chocolate, spread it on chocolate wafer cookies and top with a dollop of raspberry jam for a quick dessert.

ACTIVE TIME: 35 minutes

TOTAL: 35 minutes

PER SERVING:

307 calories; 13 g fat (3 g sat, 7 g mono); 5 mg cholesterol; 17 g carbohydrate; 11 g protein; 2 g fiber; 492 mg sodium; 641 mg potassium.

NUTRITION BONUS:

Vitamin A (103% daily value), Calcium (23% dv), Potassium (18% dv), Iron (15% dv).

H✶W   H♥H

Tofu au Vin

Here's a vegetarian take on the classic French dish coq au vin, *which is traditionally made with chicken and mushrooms and simmered in red wine. For the best texture, take your time browning the tofu. Serve with whole-wheat egg noodles and broccoli rabe or sautéed spinach.*

1   14-ounce package extra-firm tofu, drained
2   tablespoons extra-virgin olive oil, divided
1   tablespoon balsamic vinegar
¾   teaspoon salt, divided
½   teaspoon freshly ground pepper, divided
1   cup frozen pearl onions, thawed
2   medium carrots, halved lengthwise and sliced
2   cloves garlic, minced
1   bay leaf
8   ounces mushrooms, sliced
2   tablespoons plus 1 teaspoon all-purpose flour
2   cups light- to medium-bodied red wine, such as Beaujolais Nouveau, Merlot *or* Pinot Noir
2   teaspoons butter

1. Cut tofu into ½- to ¾-inch cubes and pat dry. Heat 1 tablespoon oil in a large nonstick skillet over medium-high heat. Add the tofu and cook in a single layer, stirring every 1 to 2 minutes, until golden brown, 7 to 9 minutes total. Transfer the tofu to a shallow dish big enough so it fits in one layer. Sprinkle with vinegar, ¼ teaspoon salt and ¼ teaspoon pepper; gently toss to combine.

2. Heat the remaining 1 tablespoon oil in the pan over medium heat. Add onions, carrots, garlic and bay leaf and cook, stirring often, until the vegetables are beginning to soften, about 3 minutes. Add mushrooms and cook, stirring, until they release their liquid, 3 to 5 minutes more. Sprinkle the vegetables with flour; stir to coat.

3. Add wine, the remaining ½ teaspoon salt and ¼ teaspoon pepper and cook, stirring, until the wine has reduced slightly and the sauce has thickened, 5 to 6 minutes more. Return the tofu to the pan, add butter and stir until heated through, 1 to 2 minutes. Discard the bay leaf before serving.

MAKES 4 SERVINGS, ABOUT 1 CUP EACH.

ACTIVE TIME: 30 minutes

TOTAL: 3 to 4 hours

TO MAKE AHEAD: Prepare fennel, carrot, shallot and garlic. Combine broth, 1 cup water and wine. Refrigerate in separate covered containers for up to 1 day.

EQUIPMENT: 4-quart or larger slow cooker

PER SERVING:

235 calories; 5 g fat (2 g sat, 1 g mono); 6 mg cholesterol; 36 g carbohydrate; 9 g protein; 8 g fiber; 750 mg sodium; 466 mg potassium.

NUTRITION BONUS:

Vitamin A (35% daily value), Vitamin C (15% dv).

H✖W   H⬆F   H❤H

NOTE:

Chicken-flavored broth, a vegetarian broth despite its name, is preferable to vegetable broth in some recipes for its hearty, rich flavor. Sometimes called "no-chicken" broth, it can be found with the soups in the natural-foods section of most supermarkets.

·······SAVE·······

Most types of barley and rice can be purchased in bulk at natural-foods markets and some supermarkets. The prices are often better than for packaged grains and you can buy exactly what you need for a recipe so you don't end up with leftover amounts that are hard to use up.

Barley Risotto with Fennel

This delicious take on risotto is made with barley instead of arborio rice and uses a slow cooker to make it easy. The gentle, uniform heat of a slow cooker allows you to cook this creamy risotto, seasoned with Parmesan cheese, lemon zest and oil-cured olives, without the usual frequent stirring. (Photograph: page 14.)

2	teaspoons fennel seeds
1	large *or* 2 small fennel bulbs, cored and finely diced, plus 2 tablespoons chopped fronds
1	cup pearl barley *or* short-grain brown rice
1	small carrot, finely chopped
1	large shallot, finely chopped
2	cloves garlic, minced
4	cups "no-chicken" broth (*see Note*) *or* reduced-sodium chicken broth
1-1½	cups water, divided
⅓	cup dry white wine
2	cups frozen French-cut green beans
½	cup grated Parmesan cheese
⅓	cup pitted oil-cured black olives, coarsely chopped
1	tablespoon freshly grated lemon zest
	Freshly ground pepper to taste

1. Coat a 4-quart or larger slow cooker with cooking spray. Crush fennel seeds with the bottom of a saucepan. Combine the fennel seeds, diced fennel, barley (or rice), carrot, shallot and garlic in the slow cooker. Add broth, 1 cup water and wine, and stir to combine. Cover and cook until the barley (or rice) is tender, but pleasantly chewy, and the risotto is thick and creamy, 2½ hours on high or 3½ hours on low.

2. Shortly before serving, cook green beans according to package instructions and drain. Turn off the slow cooker. Stir the green beans, Parmesan, olives, lemon zest and pepper into the risotto. If it seems dry, heat the remaining ½ cup water and stir it into the risotto. Serve sprinkled with the chopped fennel fronds.

MAKES 6 SERVINGS, GENEROUS 1 CUP EACH.

Black Bean Croquettes with Fresh Salsa

ACTIVE TIME: 25 minutes

TOTAL: 45 minutes

PER SERVING:

405 calories; 13 g fat (2 g sat, 8 g mono); 0 mg cholesterol; 61 g carbohydrate; 16 g protein; 17 g fiber; 438 mg sodium; 1,160 mg potassium.

NUTRITION BONUS:

Folate (52% daily value), Vitamin C (40% dv), Potassium (33% dv), Iron (29% dv), Vitamin A (25% dv).

With just a couple pantry items and a few fresh vegetables you can whip up these easy croquettes with fresh salsa on the side. If tomatoes are out of season they can often be expensive and flavorless. A good rule of thumb: if it doesn't smell like a tomato, it won't taste like one either. In that case, you can make the salsa with drained canned diced tomatoes. Serve with warm corn tortillas, coleslaw and lime wedges.

2	15-ounce cans black beans, rinsed, *or* 3½ cups cooked (*see How to Cook Beans, page 191*)
1	teaspoon ground cumin
1	cup frozen corn kernels, thawed
¼	cup plus ⅓ cup plain dry breadcrumbs (*see Note, page 198*), divided
2	cups finely chopped tomatoes
2	scallions, sliced
¼	cup chopped fresh cilantro
1	teaspoon chili powder, hot if desired, divided
¼	teaspoon salt
1	tablespoon extra-virgin olive oil
1	avocado, diced

1. Preheat oven to 425°F. Coat a baking sheet with cooking spray.

2. Mash black beans and cumin with a fork in a large bowl until no whole beans remain. Stir in corn and ¼ cup breadcrumbs. Combine tomatoes, scallions, cilantro, ½ teaspoon chili powder and salt in a medium bowl. Stir 1 cup of the tomato mixture into the black bean mixture.

3. Mix the remaining ⅓ cup breadcrumbs, the remaining ½ teaspoon chili powder and oil in a small bowl until the breadcrumbs are coated with oil. Divide the bean mixture into 8 scant ½-cup balls. Lightly press each bean ball into the breadcrumb mixture, turning to coat. Place on the prepared baking sheet.

4. Bake until the croquettes are heated through and the breadcrumbs are golden brown, about 20 minutes. Stir avocado into the remaining tomato mixture. Serve the salsa with the croquettes.

MAKES 4 SERVINGS, 2 CROQUETTES & ½ CUP SALSA EACH.

Huevos Rancheros Verdes

Huevos rancheros, or "ranch eggs," is a classic Mexican dish that is great for a quick dinner. For about 25 cents each, it's hard to beat the nutritional value of an egg, and here they are combined with another inexpensive superfood—beans. Traditionally the dish is made with a red tomato-based sauce, but here we use tart and tangy green salsa instead. Serve with brown rice and slices of avocado.

1 ½   cups very thinly sliced romaine lettuce
1   scallion, sliced
2   tablespoons chopped fresh cilantro
3   teaspoons canola oil, divided
2   teaspoons lime juice
¼   teaspoon salt, divided
¼   teaspoon freshly ground pepper, divided
1   15-ounce can pinto beans, rinsed, *or* 1 ⅓ cups cooked (*see How to Cook Beans, page 191*)
¼   cup prepared green salsa (*see Note*)
8   6-inch corn tortillas
      Canola oil cooking spray
¾   cup shredded sharp Cheddar cheese
4   large eggs

1. Preheat oven to 400°F.

2. Combine lettuce, scallion, cilantro, 1 teaspoon oil, lime juice, ⅛ teaspoon salt and ⅛ teaspoon pepper in a bowl; set aside. Combine beans and salsa in another bowl.

3. Coat both sides of each tortilla with cooking spray. Place tortillas on a large baking sheet in 4 sets of overlapping pairs. (Each pair should overlap by about 3 inches.) Spread about ⅓ cup of the bean mixture on top of each pair of tortillas and sprinkle with 3 tablespoons cheese each. Bake until the beans are hot and the cheese is melted, about 10 minutes.

4. Meanwhile, heat the remaining 2 teaspoons oil in a large nonstick skillet over medium heat. Crack each egg into a small bowl and slip them one at a time into the pan, taking care not to break the yolks. Season the eggs with the remaining ⅛ teaspoon salt and pepper. Reduce heat to medium-low and cook undisturbed for 5 to 7 minutes for soft-set yolks. (For hard-set yolks, cover the pan after 5 minutes and continue cooking until the yolks are cooked through, 4 to 6 minutes more.)

5. To assemble, place an egg on top of each pair of tortillas and top with a generous ¼ cup of the lettuce mixture.

MAKES 4 SERVINGS.

ACTIVE TIME: 30 minutes

TOTAL: 30 minutes

PER SERVING:

396 calories; 18 g fat (6 g sat, 5 g mono); 234 mg cholesterol; 42 g carbohydrate; 20 g protein; 8 g fiber; 562 mg sodium; 471 mg potassium.

NUTRITION BONUS:

Vitamin A (40% daily value), Folate (29% dv), Calcium (27% dv), Iron & Magnesium (18% dv).

H✖W   H⬆F

NOTE:

Green salsa (sometimes labeled salsa verde or tomatillo salsa) is made with tomatillos, green chiles and onions. Look for it near other prepared salsa in large supermarkets.

4

CHICKEN & TURKEY

Poultry often goes on sale, so when it does, stock up and keep it in your freezer. Also, learn to cook whole chickens, thighs and drumsticks—not just boneless, skinless chicken breast, which tends to be more expensive.

Crispy Chicken Tostadas (*page 84*)

ACTIVE TIME: 35 minutes

TOTAL: 35 minutes

PER SERVING:

422 calories; 17 g fat (5 g sat, 8 g mono); 88 mg cholesterol; 34 g carbohydrate; 34 g protein; 8 g fiber; 678 mg sodium; 698 mg potassium.

NUTRITION BONUS:

Vitamin A (27% daily value), Magnesium (21% dv), Potassium (20% dv), Calcium & Vitamin C (19% dv), Folate (17% dv), Zinc (16% dv).

H↑F H♥H

NOTE:

To poach **chicken breasts**, place boneless, skinless chicken breasts in a medium skillet or saucepan. Figure 4 ounces raw chicken for each 1 cup shredded or diced cooked chicken. Add lightly salted water to cover and bring to a boil. Cover, reduce heat to low and simmer gently until chicken is cooked through and no longer pink in the middle, 10 to 15 minutes.

···········SAVE···········

Turn leftover corn tortillas into chips for snacks. Cut them into wedges, coat them with cooking spray, spread on a baking sheet and bake in a 375°F oven, turning once, until crispy, about 10 minutes.

Crispy Chicken Tostadas

Use leftover chicken or turkey to top these homemade tostadas. You could even use chopped-up roast pork in this Tex-Mex favorite. Making your own tostada shells from fresh corn tortillas is easier than you might think—crisp them in the oven while you prepare the toppings. Serve with black beans, rice and extra salsa or hot sauce on the side. (Photograph: page 82.)

1	14-ounce can petite diced tomatoes, preferably with jalapeños
1	medium onion, thinly sliced
3	cups shredded cooked chicken *or* turkey (12 ounces; *see Note*)
8	6-inch corn tortillas
	Canola *or* olive oil cooking spray
1	avocado, pitted
¼	cup prepared salsa
2	tablespoons reduced-fat sour cream
2	tablespoons chopped fresh cilantro
1	cup shredded romaine lettuce
½	cup shredded Monterey Jack cheese

1. Position racks in upper and lower thirds of oven; preheat to 375°F.

2. Bring tomatoes and their juice to a boil in a medium saucepan over medium heat. Add onion and cook, stirring occasionally, until the onion is soft and most of the liquid has evaporated, 15 to 20 minutes. Add chicken (or turkey) and cook until heated through, 1 to 2 minutes.

3. Meanwhile, coat tortillas on both sides with cooking spray. Divide the tortillas between 2 large baking sheets. Bake, turning once, until crisped and lightly browned, about 10 minutes.

4. Mash avocado in a bowl. Stir in salsa, sour cream and cilantro until combined.

5. To assemble tostadas, spread each crisped tortilla with some of the avocado mixture. Top with the chicken (or turkey) mixture, lettuce and cheese.

MAKES 4 SERVINGS, 2 TOSTADAS EACH.

Simple Roast Chicken

There's no reason to get overly fussy with complicated techniques for a simple roast chicken, the ultimate comfort food. You can also take comfort in the fact that buying the whole bird is the cheapest way to go. Plus, with the leftover meat and bones you can make chicken broth to use in soup (see page 190). *That's triple comfort!* (Photograph: page 10.)

ACTIVE TIME: 15 minutes

TOTAL: 2 hours 20 minutes

EQUIPMENT: Kitchen string

PER 3-OUNCE SERVING
(WITHOUT SKIN):

180 calories; 9 g fat (2 g sat, 5 g mono); 64 mg cholesterol; 1 g carbohydrate; 21 g protein; 0 g fiber; 359 mg sodium; 217 mg potassium.

- 1 small onion, peeled and quartered
- 3 cloves garlic, peeled and quartered
- 3 sprigs fresh tarragon
- 3 sprigs fresh thyme
- 1 5-pound chicken, giblets removed
- 2 tablespoons extra-virgin olive oil
- 1 teaspoon kosher salt
- ½ teaspoon freshly ground pepper

1. Preheat oven to 375°F.

2. Place onion, garlic, tarragon and thyme into the chicken cavity. Tie the legs together with kitchen string, mostly closing the cavity opening. Pull the wings so the tips overlap on top of the breast; tie in place, wrapping string around the wings and body. Rub the chicken with oil, salt and pepper. Set in a roasting pan, breast-side down.

3. Roast the chicken for 25 minutes. Turn breast-side up and continue roasting, basting occasionally with pan juices, until a thermometer inserted into the thickest part of the thigh, without touching bone, registers 165°F, 1¼ to 1½ hours. Transfer to a cutting board; let rest for 10 minutes. Remove the string before carving.

MAKES 8 SERVINGS.

ACTIVE TIME: 15 minutes

TOTAL: 1 ¾ hours

EQUIPMENT: Kitchen string, metal or foil drip pan

PER 3-OUNCE SERVING (WITHOUT SKIN):

173 calories; 7 g fat (2 g sat, 2 g mono); 76 mg cholesterol; 2 g carbohydrate; 25 g protein; 1 g fiber; 656 mg sodium; 250 mg potassium.

H✖W   H♥H

NOTE:

Smoked paprika and **ground chipotle chile** can be found in the spice section of well-stocked supermarkets or online at *penzeys.com*.

Beer-Barbecued Chicken

Here's our spin on the roast-a-chicken-on-top-of-a-can-of-beer technique that's popular with barbecue aficionados. The beer keeps the meat juicy and a smoky-flavored spice rub both under and over the skin gives it extra flavor. To keep calories and fat in check, remove the skin before serving.

1	tablespoon smoked paprika (*see Note*)
2	teaspoons dried oregano
1 ½	teaspoons salt
1	teaspoon packed dark brown sugar
1	teaspoon ground cumin
½	teaspoon onion powder
½	teaspoon garlic powder
½	teaspoon ground chipotle chile (*see Note*)
½	teaspoon freshly ground pepper
1	4-pound chicken, giblets removed
1	12-ounce bottle beer, preferably pale ale *or* American lager, divided

1. Preheat a gas grill (with all burners lit) to 400°F or build a fire in a charcoal grill and let it burn down to medium heat (about 400°F).

2. Combine paprika, oregano, salt, brown sugar, cumin, onion powder, garlic powder, chipotle chile and pepper in a small bowl.

3. Trim any excess skin from chicken. Loosen the skin over the breast and thigh meat. Rub the spice mixture under the skin onto the breast meat and leg meat, a little on the skin and inside the cavity. Tuck the wings under the body and tie the legs together with kitchen string.

4. If using a gas grill, turn off one burner (leaving 1 to 2 burners lit, depending on your grill). If using a charcoal grill, move the coals to one side. Wearing an oven mitt, carefully place a drip pan under the grill rack on the unheated side. Place the chicken breast-side down on the rack over the pan. Pour half the beer into the cavity (it's OK if some drips out into the pan).

5. Close the lid and roast undisturbed for 45 minutes.

6. Turn the chicken breast-side up. Pour the remaining beer into the cavity. Cover and continue roasting until an instant-read thermometer inserted into the thickest part of the thigh, without touching bone, registers 165°F, 30 to 45 minutes more. Transfer the chicken to a clean cutting board; let rest for 10 minutes. Remove the string before carving.

MAKES 6 SERVINGS.

Quick Roast Chicken & Root Vegetables

Roasted chicken in 45 minutes? No problem. This technique of starting bone-in chicken breasts on the stovetop and finishing them in a hot oven with vegetables gets a hearty dinner on the table in a hurry. While everything roasts, you still have time to make a quick pan sauce with shallot and Dijon mustard. Serve with a spinach salad.

ACTIVE TIME: 45 minutes

TOTAL: 45 minutes

PER SERVING:

333 calories; 10 g fat (2 g sat, 6 g mono); 72 mg cholesterol; 29 g carbohydrate; 31 g protein; 4 g fiber; 770 mg sodium; 1,033 mg potassium.

NUTRITION BONUS:

Vitamin C (60% daily value), Potassium (30% dv), Magnesium (17% dv).

H✱W   H♥H

1 pound turnips, peeled and cut into ½-inch chunks
1 pound baby potatoes, quartered
2 tablespoons extra-virgin olive oil, divided
1 tablespoon chopped fresh marjoram *or* 1 teaspoon dried
¾ teaspoon salt, divided
½ teaspoon freshly ground pepper, divided
¼ cup all-purpose flour
1 cup reduced-sodium chicken broth
2 bone-in chicken breasts (12 ounces each), skin and fat removed, cut in half crosswise
1 large shallot, chopped
1 tablespoon Dijon mustard
2 teaspoons red- *or* white-wine vinegar

1. Preheat oven to 500°F.

2. Toss turnips, potatoes, 1 tablespoon oil, marjoram, ½ teaspoon salt and ¼ teaspoon pepper together in a medium bowl. Spread in an even layer on a large baking sheet. Roast for 15 minutes.

3. Meanwhile, place flour in a shallow dish. Transfer 2 teaspoons of the flour to a small bowl and whisk in broth; set aside. Season chicken with the remaining ¼ teaspoon each salt and pepper. Dredge the chicken in the flour, shaking off excess. (Discard any leftover flour.)

4. Heat the remaining 1 tablespoon oil in a large skillet over medium heat. Add the chicken, skinned-side down, and cook until well browned on the bottom, about 5 minutes. Remove from the heat.

5. After the vegetables have been roasting for 15 minutes, stir them and place one piece of chicken, skinned-side up, in each corner of the baking sheet. (Set the skillet aside.) Return the vegetables and chicken to the oven and roast until the chicken is cooked through (an instant-read thermometer inserted into the thickest part of the meat registers 165°F) and the vegetables are tender, about 20 minutes more.

6. When the chicken and vegetables have about 10 minutes left, return the skillet to medium heat. Add shallot and cook, stirring, until fragrant, about 1 minute. Whisk the reserved broth mixture again, add to the pan and bring to a boil. Cook, stirring occasionally, until reduced by about half, about 8 minutes. Stir in mustard and vinegar. Serve the chicken and vegetables with the sauce.

MAKES 4 SERVINGS.

⋯⋯ S A V E ⋯⋯⋯⋯⋯⋯⋯⋯⋯⋯

Use root vegetables interchangeably. This recipe calls for turnips and baby potatoes, but you could use carrots, parsnips or beets if you have those on hand. Just cut them into equal sizes so they cook evenly.

ACTIVE TIME: 40 minutes

TOTAL: 40 minutes

PER SERVING:

255 calories; 8 g fat (2 g sat, 3 g mono); 93 mg cholesterol; 16 g carbohydrate; 29 g protein; 1 g fiber; 389 mg sodium; 315 mg potassium.

NUTRITION BONUS:

Zinc (22% daily value), Vitamin C (15% dv).

BROILER VARIATION:

Position oven rack in the upper third of the oven; preheat broiler to high. Prepare sauce (Step 2). Coat a broiler pan with cooking spray. Sprinkle drumsticks with salt and pepper (Step 3), then broil, turning once, until an instant-read thermometer inserted into the thickest part registers 165°F, about 15 minutes total.

SAVE

Chicken drumsticks often cost less than a dollar a pound and are delicious grilled or roasted. For an even better value, look for family-size packages of frozen drumsticks.

Sweet-&-Sour Chicken Drumsticks

These grilled drumsticks stay deliciously moist—even with the skin removed. Our minty sweet-and-sour dipping sauce adds a refreshing twist to this crowd-pleasing grilled chicken dish. Serve with brown rice and slices of fresh pineapple.

½	teaspoon freshly grated orange zest
¼	cup orange juice
¼	cup water
3	tablespoons honey
1	tablespoon plus 1 teaspoon cider vinegar, divided
½	teaspoon salt, divided
¼	teaspoon ground coriander
1	teaspoon cornstarch
¼	cup chopped fresh mint
8	chicken drumsticks (about 2 pounds), skin removed, trimmed
¼	teaspoon freshly ground pepper

1. Preheat grill to medium. (*No grill? See Broiler Variation, left.*)

2. **To prepare dipping sauce:** Combine orange zest, orange juice, water, honey, 1 tablespoon vinegar, ¼ teaspoon salt and coriander in a small saucepan; bring to a boil. Whisk cornstarch and the remaining 1 teaspoon vinegar in a small bowl until smooth. Add to the saucepan and return to a boil, whisking until thickened, 30 seconds to 1 minute. Remove from the heat. Stir in mint.

3. Sprinkle drumsticks with the remaining ¼ teaspoon salt and pepper. Oil the grill rack (*see Note, page 200*). Grill the drumsticks until crispy on all sides and an instant-read thermometer inserted into the thickest part without touching bone registers 165°F, about 15 minutes total. Serve the drumsticks with the dipping sauce on the side.

MAKES 4 SERVINGS.

Chicken in Garlic-Vinegar Sauce

Braising chicken in vinegar and herbs is a popular way of cooking in Mediterranean Europe. Often paired with sweet sausage, this is a gutsy, hearty dish. It's delicious made a day ahead. Serve with whole-wheat couscous tossed with fresh herbs and steamed broccolini.

ACTIVE TIME: 1 hour

TOTAL: 1 hour 50 minutes

TO MAKE AHEAD: Prepare through Step 3; cool to room temperature and refrigerate for up to 1 day. Finish with Steps 4-5 before serving.

PER SERVING:

301 calories; 14 g fat (5 g sat, 6 g mono); 116 mg cholesterol; 9 g carbohydrate; 34 g protein; 1 g fiber; 361 mg sodium; 612 mg potassium.

NUTRITION BONUS:

Vitamin C (20% daily value), Potassium & Zinc (17% dv), Vitamin A (15% dv).

H ✖ W

NOTE:

If you are using a combination of **thighs, drumsticks and breasts**, cut each breast in half crosswise to make pieces about the size of a thigh. And if you buy whole legs, separate the drumsticks and thighs. When the pieces are about the same size, they'll cook at about the same rate

3-3½	pounds bone-in chicken pieces (thighs, drumsticks *and/or* breasts), skin removed, trimmed (*see Note*)
½	teaspoon coarse salt, plus a pinch, divided
½	teaspoon freshly ground pepper
7	teaspoons extra-virgin olive oil, divided
1	tablespoon butter
½	cup minced shallots
16	large cloves garlic, peeled
⅓	cup sherry vinegar *or* red-wine vinegar
1	cup reduced-sodium chicken broth
2	sprigs fresh thyme *or* 2 teaspoons dried
½	cup reduced-fat sour cream
1	tablespoon Dijon mustard
2	teaspoons tomato paste
2	teaspoons all-purpose flour
2	medium tomatoes, seeded and cut into ½-inch pieces
2	tablespoons finely minced fresh chives

1. Pat chicken pieces dry with paper towels and season with ½ teaspoon salt and pepper. Heat 2 teaspoons oil and butter in a large heavy casserole or Dutch oven over medium heat. Add half the chicken pieces and cook, turning occasionally, until browned on all sides, 5 to 7 minutes. Remove to a large plate. Repeat with another 2 teaspoons oil and the remaining chicken.

2. Heat 2 more teaspoons oil in the pot. Add shallots and garlic and cook, stirring, until the shallots are soft and lightly browned, about 1 minute. Add vinegar and bring to a simmer. Return the chicken to the pot. Pour in broth and then carefully nestle the thyme sprigs among the chicken pieces (or stir in dry thyme).

3. Cover the pot with a tight-fitting lid and simmer over medium-low heat until the chicken is very tender, about 50 minutes.

4. Just before the chicken is done, whisk sour cream, mustard, tomato paste and flour in a small bowl until smooth. Combine tomatoes, chives, the remaining 1 teaspoon oil and pinch of salt in another small bowl; reserve for garnish.

5. When the chicken is done, remove to a plate, discarding the thyme sprigs (if using). Stir the sour cream mixture into the sauce; bring to a simmer. Reduce heat to low, return the chicken to the sauce and reheat, about 1 minute. Serve garnished with the tomato mixture.

MAKES 6 SERVINGS.

ACTIVE TIME: 40 minutes

TOTAL: 4 1/2 hours

TO MAKE AHEAD: Prepare through Step 4 up to adding the peas and parsley. Cover and refrigerate for up to 2 days or freeze for up to 3 months. Thaw in the refrigerator, if necessary, and reheat; just before serving, stir in peas and parsley.

EQUIPMENT: 5- to 6-quart slow cooker

PER SERVING:

323 calories; 15 g fat (5 g sat, 6 g mono); 99 mg cholesterol; 16 g carbohydrate; 31 g protein; 3 g fiber; 701 mg sodium; 857 mg potassium.

NUTRITION BONUS:

Vitamin A (100% daily value), Vitamin C (33% dv), Zinc (26% dv), Potassium (24% dv), Iron (17% dv).

H✂W   H♥H

SIMMERED STEW VARIATION:

TOTAL: 1 1/2 hours

In Step 1, use only 1 1/2 cups broth. In Step 2, add chicken, lemon slices and lemon zest to the Dutch oven. Cover and simmer gently over low heat until the chicken is very tender, about 45 minutes. Discard lemon slices and bay leaves. Omit Step 3. Continue with Step 4, cooking everything in the Dutch oven over medium-high heat.

Rich Chicken Stew

An infatuation with the virtuousness of boneless, skinless chicken breast often eclipses the fact that dark meat is moist and tender, provides more iron and costs a lot less. Plus, it can easily be argued that thighs are way more flavorful. Here they are used in a lightened-up, slow-cooker version of a blanquette, *which is a classic French stew of veal, chicken or lamb with mushrooms in a velvety sauce. Just a little whipping cream (which is less inclined to break down than lighter creams and gives more density to the sauce) adds richness. This is delightful over egg noodles.* (Photograph: page 14.)

1	pound mushrooms, stems trimmed, caps wiped clean	1/2	teaspoon freshly grated lemon zest
1/2	cup finely chopped shallots (2 large)	2	1/4-inch-thick lemon slices (including peel), seeded
2	teaspoons extra-virgin olive oil	2	tablespoons cornstarch
1/2	cup water, divided	1/4	cup whipping cream
4	cups reduced-sodium chicken broth	2	tablespoons lemon juice
1	cup thinly sliced carrot	1/2	teaspoon salt
1	teaspoon fresh thyme leaves *or* 1/2 teaspoon dried		Freshly ground pepper to taste
2	bay leaves	1 1/2	cups frozen green peas, thawed
2	pounds boneless, skinless chicken thighs, trimmed and cut into 2-inch chunks	1/2	cup chopped fresh parsley

1. Combine mushrooms, shallots, oil and 1/4 cup water in a 5- to 6-quart Dutch oven. Cover and cook over high heat, stirring often, until mushrooms are juicy, 3 to 4 minutes. Uncover and cook, stirring often, until the mushrooms are lightly browned, 8 to 10 minutes. Add broth, carrot, thyme and bay leaves; bring to a boil.

2. Place chicken in a 5- to 6-quart slow cooker (*or see Variation, left*). Lay lemon slices on top. Turn heat to high. Carefully pour in the vegetable mixture. Cover and cook until the chicken is very tender, 3 1/2 to 4 hours.

3. With a slotted spoon, transfer the chicken and vegetables to a bowl; discard bay leaves and lemon slices. Skim fat and pour the juices into a large saucepan; add lemon zest. Bring to a boil over high heat. Boil until reduced to 2 cups, 15 to 20 minutes.

4. Mix cornstarch with remaining 1/4 cup water in a small bowl. Add to the pan and cook, stirring, until slightly thickened. Add cream and lemon juice; stir until boiling. Return the chicken and vegetables to the sauce and heat through. Season with salt and pepper. Just before serving, stir in peas and parsley.

MAKES 6 SERVINGS, ABOUT 1 CUP EACH.

Chicken & Sweet Potato Stew

Bone-in chicken thighs are delicious and one of the best values in the poultry section of the market. Here, they are combined with those nutritional dynamos, sweet potatoes, in a hearty slow-cooker stew that's designed for that cool day when you'd rather be outside raking the leaves from the garden, getting it ready for what's ahead, than slaving over the stove. (Photograph: page 14.)

6	bone-in chicken thighs, skin removed, trimmed (*see Note*)
2	pounds sweet potatoes, peeled and cut into spears
8	ounces white button mushrooms, thinly sliced
6	large shallots, peeled and halved
4	cloves garlic, peeled
1	cup dry white wine
2	teaspoons chopped fresh rosemary *or* 1/2 teaspoon dried, crushed
1	teaspoon salt
1/2	teaspoon freshly ground pepper
1 1/2	tablespoons white-wine vinegar

Place chicken, sweet potatoes, mushrooms, shallots, garlic, wine, rosemary, salt and pepper in a 5- to 6-quart slow cooker; stir to combine. Put the lid on and cook on low until the sweet potatoes are tender, about 5 hours. Before serving, remove bones from the chicken, if desired, and stir in vinegar.

MAKES 6 SERVINGS.

ACTIVE TIME: 20 minutes

TOTAL: 5 hours 20 minutes

TO MAKE AHEAD: Cover and refrigerate for up to 3 days or freeze for up to 1 month.

EQUIPMENT: 5- to 6-quart slow cooker

PER SERVING:

301 calories; 6 g fat (2 g sat, 2 g mono); 50 mg cholesterol; 38 g carbohydrate; 18 g protein; 5 g fiber; 521 mg sodium; 892 mg potassium.

NUTRITION BONUS:

Vitamin A (440% daily value), Potassium (25% dv), Magnesium & Zinc (15% dv).

NOTE:

To trim boneless, skinless **chicken thighs**, use kitchen shears to snip the fat away from the meat.

ACTIVE TIME: 40 minutes

TOTAL: 40 minutes

PER SERVING:

366 calories; 15 g fat (3 g sat, 8 g mono); 85 mg cholesterol; 20 g carbohydrate; 25 g protein; 1 g fiber; 445 mg sodium; 274 mg potassium.

NUTRITION BONUS:

Zinc (17% daily value).

H ♥ H

NOTES:

To trim boneless, skinless **chicken thighs**, use kitchen shears to snip the fat away from the meat.

Port is a fortified wine that provides depth of flavor in cooking. Look for it at a liquor store or in the wine section of the supermarket.

Chicken Thighs with Green Olive, Cherry & Port Sauce

 A sweet-and-savory dried cherry sauce with port turns humble, inexpensive chicken thighs into a succulent dish that's special enough for company. It's also great with lean pork or chicken breast. Substitute cranberry juice for the port if you prefer. Serve with bulgur tossed with chopped pistachios and fresh herbs and steamed green beans.

1 ½	pounds boneless, skinless chicken thighs, trimmed (*see Notes*)
¼	teaspoon salt
¼	teaspoon freshly ground pepper
¼	cup all-purpose flour
¾	cup port (*see Notes*) or cranberry juice cocktail, divided
1	tablespoon plus 1 teaspoon extra-virgin olive oil, divided
4	cloves garlic, minced
¾	cup reduced-sodium chicken broth
¼	cup dried cherries *or* dried cranberries
¼	cup sliced pitted green olives
2	tablespoons red-wine vinegar
1	tablespoon brown sugar
1	teaspoon dried oregano

1. Season chicken with salt and pepper. Place flour in a shallow dish. Add chicken and turn to coat. Measure out 4 teaspoons of the flour to a small bowl and whisk in ¼ cup port (or cranberry juice cocktail) until smooth. (Discard the remaining flour.)

2. Heat 1 tablespoon oil in a large nonstick skillet over medium heat. Add the chicken and cook until browned on the outside and no longer pink in the middle, about 4 minutes per side. Transfer to a plate.

3. Add the remaining 1 teaspoon oil and garlic to the pan; cook, stirring, until fragrant, about 30 seconds. Add the flour mixture, the remaining ½ cup port (or juice), broth, dried cherries (or cranberries), olives, vinegar, brown sugar and oregano. Bring to a boil, stirring. Reduce heat to a simmer and cook, stirring occasionally, until the sauce has thickened, 4 to 6 minutes.

4. Return the chicken to the pan along with any accumulated juices. Turn to coat with sauce and cook until heated through, about 2 minutes. Serve the chicken with the sauce.

MAKES 4 SERVINGS.

Chicken with Honey-Orange Sauce

Here we combine raisins, cinnamon, honey and almonds with orange juice, zest, wine and broth to make a rich, savory pan sauce for chicken. If you want to use up orange juice that's sitting in your refrigerator, use about ¼ cup instead of the fresh-squeezed and skip the zest. There's plenty of the gorgeous sauce, so be sure to serve whole-wheat egg noodles, couscous or rice on the side.

2	navel oranges
2	tablespoons all-purpose flour
½	teaspoon salt, divided
¼	teaspoon freshly ground pepper
4	boneless, skinless chicken breasts (about 1 ¼ pounds), trimmed and tenders removed (*see Note, page 200*)
1	cup reduced-sodium chicken broth
1	tablespoon canola oil
1	cup white wine
½	cup golden raisins
2	tablespoons honey
1	3 inch cinnamon stick
½	cup slivered almonds, toasted (*see Note*)

1. Zest and juice one orange. Peel the other orange, remove the white pith, then halve and slice. Reserve the orange slices separately from the zest and juice.

2. Combine flour, ¼ teaspoon salt and pepper in a shallow dish. Dredge chicken in the flour, shaking off any excess. Transfer the remaining flour to a small bowl, add broth and whisk to combine.

3. Heat oil in a large nonstick skillet over medium heat. Add the chicken and cook until browned, 3 to 4 minutes per side. Transfer to a plate. Add wine to the pan and cook for 1 minute. Add the flour-broth mixture, the reserved orange zest and juice, the remaining ¼ teaspoon salt, raisins, honey and cinnamon stick; bring to a boil. Reduce heat to a simmer, return the chicken and any accumulated juices to the pan and cook, turning the chicken once or twice, until an instant-read thermometer inserted into the thickest part of the meat registers 165°F and the sauce has thickened, 10 to 12 minutes.

4. Transfer the chicken to a serving platter. Discard the cinnamon stick. Spoon the sauce over the chicken and garnish with the reserved orange slices and almonds.

MAKES 4 SERVINGS.

ACTIVE TIME: 35 minutes

TOTAL: 35 minutes

PER SERVING:

418 calories; 12 g fat (2 g sat, 7 g mono); 72 mg cholesterol; 37 g carbohydrate; 31 g protein; 3 g fiber; 498 mg sodium; 638 mg potassium.

NUTRITION BONUS:

Vitamin C (55% daily value), Magnesium (19% dv), Potassium (18% dv).

H ♥ H

NOTE:

To toast **slivered almonds**, cook in a small dry skillet over medium-low heat, stirring constantly, until fragrant and lightly browned, 2 to 4 minutes.

ACTIVE TIME: 20 minutes

TOTAL: 1 hour 20 minutes (including 1 hour marinating time)

TO MAKE AHEAD: Cover and refrigerate the sauce for up to 1 week.

PER SERVING:

296 calories; 4 g fat (1 g sat, 3 g mono); 66 mg cholesterol; 36 g carbohydrate; 27 g protein; 0 g fiber; 371 mg sodium; 370 mg potassium.

H)(W   H ♥ H

NOTE:

It's difficult to find an individual **chicken breast** small enough for one portion. Removing the thin strip of meat from the underside of a 5- to 6-ounce breast—the "tender"—removes about 1 ounce of meat and yields a perfect individual portion. Wrap and freeze the tenders and when you have gathered enough, use them in a stir-fry.

Raspberry-Balsamic Chicken with Shallots

Tasty and flexible—what more could you want in a recipe? You could easily vary the flavors (and make use of what you have in your pantry) by making the dish with black cherry jam and red-wine vinegar, apricot jam and cider vinegar or orange marmalade and sherry vinegar. Plus, if you like, the dish can be prepared with thrifty boneless, skinless chicken thighs.

¾	cup seedless all-fruit raspberry jam
¼	cup balsamic vinegar
½	teaspoon salt
¼	teaspoon freshly ground pepper
4	boneless, skinless chicken breasts (about 1¼ pounds), trimmed and tenders removed (*see Note*)
2½	teaspoons extra-virgin olive oil
½	cup chopped shallots (2-3 large)
1½	teaspoons minced fresh thyme *or* ½ teaspoon dried

1. Combine jam and vinegar in a small pan over medium-low heat. Cook, stirring often, until the jam is dissolved, 3 to 4 minutes. Remove from heat, stir in salt and pepper and let cool slightly. Reserve ½ cup of the sauce. Place chicken breasts and the rest of the sauce in a large sealable plastic bag. Seal and shake gently to coat. Marinate in the refrigerator for 1 to 1½ hours.

2. Heat oil in a large nonstick skillet over medium-high heat. Add shallots and thyme and cook, stirring often, until the shallots begin to soften, about 1 minute. Remove the chicken from the marinade (discard marinade). Add the chicken to the pan and cook until just beginning to brown, about 2 minutes per side. Add the reserved raspberry sauce; stir to melt the jam and coat the chicken. Reduce heat to low, cover and cook until the chicken is cooked through and no longer pink in the center, 6 to 10 minutes. Serve immediately.

MAKES 4 SERVINGS.

Stuffing-Topped Chicken

Here's a one-skillet version of chicken and stuffing made with wholesome ingredients. For the stuffing, use any bread that's no longer sandwich-perfect rather than letting it go to waste. Serve with Brussels sprouts and mashed potatoes.

2	tablespoons extra-virgin olive oil, divided
¾	cup chopped celery
1	tablespoon chopped shallot
5	slices whole-wheat country bread, cut into ¼-inch cubes
½	teaspoon salt-free poultry seasoning (*see Notes*)
1½	cups reduced-sodium chicken broth, divided
1½	pounds boneless, skinless chicken thighs, trimmed and cut into 1-inch pieces (*see Notes*)
4	tablespoons all-purpose flour, divided
½	teaspoon freshly ground pepper
¼	teaspoon salt
2½	cups quartered mushrooms (6 ounces)
⅓	cup dry white wine *or* dry sherry

1. Position rack in upper third of oven; preheat broiler.

2. Heat 1 tablespoon oil in a large ovenproof skillet over medium heat. Add celery and shallot; cook, stirring, until the shallot begins to brown, about 2 minutes. Add bread and poultry seasoning; cook, stirring, until the celery has softened and the bread begins to crisp, 2 to 3 minutes. Transfer the stuffing to a medium bowl and toss with ¼ cup broth; set aside. Wipe out the pan.

3. Toss chicken with 2 tablespoons flour, pepper and salt in a large bowl. Whisk the remaining 1¼ cups broth with the remaining 2 tablespoons flour in a small bowl and set aside.

4. Heat the remaining 1 tablespoon oil in the pan over medium heat. Add the chicken (shaking off any excess flour) and mushrooms; cook, stirring, until the chicken is cooked through, about 8 minutes.

5. Increase heat to medium-high; add wine (or sherry) and cook, scraping up any browned bits with a wooden spoon, until almost evaporated, about 2 minutes. Stir in the reserved broth-flour mixture and cook, stirring, until thickened, about 2 minutes more. Spoon the reserved stuffing over the chicken mixture. Transfer the pan to the oven and broil until the stuffing begins to crisp, about 4 minutes.

MAKES 4 SERVINGS.

ACTIVE TIME: 45 minutes

TOTAL: 45 minutes

PER SERVING:

397 calories; 17 g fat (4 g sat, 9 g mono); 76 mg cholesterol; 27 g carbohydrate; 30 g protein; 3 g fiber; 636 mg sodium; 592 mg potassium.

NUTRITION BONUS:

Zinc (22% daily value), Iron & Potassium (17% dv), Folate (16% dv), Magnesium (15% dv).

H✂W   H♥H

NOTES:

Look for **"salt-free" poultry seasoning** near other spice mixes. If you can only find poultry seasoning with salt, reduce the salt in the recipe to ⅛ teaspoon.

To trim boneless, skinless **chicken thighs**, use kitchen shears to snip the fat away from the meat.

ACTIVE TIME: 45 minutes

TOTAL: 45 minutes

TO MAKE AHEAD: Store croutons (Steps 1-2) airtight at room temperature for up to 3 days.

PER SERVING:

463 calories; 24 g fat (7 g sat, 10 g mono); 233 mg cholesterol; 37 g carbohydrate; 25 g protein; 9 g fiber; 586 mg sodium; 506 mg potassium.

NUTRITION BONUS:

Vitamin C (130% daily value), Vitamin A (110% dv), Folate (38% dv), Iron (28% dv), Magnesium (17% dv).

H ⬆ F

One-Skillet Bean & Broccoli Rabe Supper

If beans and greens are not a part of your regular menu, this one-pot dish will change your mind. The wide range of seasoning in sausage brings many flavors to the broccoli rabe and beans, so only garlic, salt and pepper need to be added to achieve a complex-tasting dish. Big, rustic croutons, which can be made from stale whole-wheat bread, soak up the broth.

3   slices whole-wheat country bread (5-6 ounces), crusts removed
2   tablespoons plus 1 teaspoon extra-virgin olive oil, divided
    Freshly ground pepper to taste
4   ounces uncooked Italian chicken, turkey *or* pork sausage links
2   cloves garlic, thinly sliced
1   bunch broccoli rabe (about 12 ounces), trimmed and coarsely chopped
2   cups cooked cannellini beans (*see How to Cook Beans, page 191*) *or* rinsed canned beans (*see Note, page 199*)
½   cup bean-cooking liquid *or* water
⅛   teaspoon salt, plus a pinch, divided
4   large eggs

1. Preheat oven to 400°F.

2. Tear bread into ½- to 1-inch irregular pieces. Place on a large baking sheet and toss with 1 tablespoon oil. Season with pepper. Bake until golden brown and crisp, 10 to 12 minutes.

3. Meanwhile, heat 1 teaspoon oil in a large skillet, preferably cast-iron, over medium heat. Remove sausage from casing and cook, breaking it up, until browned and cooked through, 3 to 5 minutes. Drain on paper towels. Let the pan cool.

4. Pour off any oil left in the pan, add the remaining 1 tablespoon oil and place over medium heat. Add garlic and cook, stirring, until fragrant, about 30 seconds. Add broccoli rabe and cook, stirring, until wilted and tender but still bright green, 4 to 6 minutes. (Add 1 to 2 tablespoons water if the greens seem dry.)

5. Add beans, bean-cooking liquid (or water), the sausage and ⅛ teaspoon salt to the pan, stirring to combine; bring to a simmer. Make 4 indentations in the bean mixture and break an egg into each one. Season the eggs with the remaining pinch of salt and pepper to taste. Cover the pan and cook the eggs, checking occasionally, until desired doneness: 3 to 5 minutes for soft-set yolks, 7 to 9 minutes for hard-set yolks.

6. Top the bean mixture and eggs with the croutons and serve immediately.

MAKES 4 SERVINGS.

Dirty Rice

A Louisiana favorite, our version of this spicy dish uses whole-grain brown rice. Traditionally made with chicken liver, which gives it a "dirty" color, we use healthy lean chicken sausage instead.

1 ½	cups long-grain brown rice
3	cups reduced-sodium chicken broth
1	tablespoon peanut oil *or* canola oil
10	ounces cooked chicken andouille *or* other spicy chicken sausage, cut into ½-inch pieces
1 ½	cups chopped yellow onion
1 ¼	cups chopped celery
1	cup chopped green bell pepper
1	cup chopped red bell pepper
2	cloves garlic, minced
2	teaspoons chopped fresh thyme *or* ¾ teaspoon dried
¼-½	teaspoon cayenne pepper
¼	teaspoon salt

1. Bring rice and broth to a boil in a large saucepan. Reduce heat to low, cover, and simmer at the lowest bubble until the water is absorbed and the rice is tender, about 50 minutes (*see Note*). Remove from the heat and let stand, covered, for 10 minutes.

2. While the rice is standing, heat oil in a large nonstick skillet over medium heat. Add sausage and cook, stirring, until it begins to brown, about 5 minutes. Add onion, celery, green and red bell pepper and garlic and cook, stirring, until the onion is soft, about 5 minutes more. Stir in thyme, cayenne to taste and salt. Stir the sausage mixture into the rice and serve.

MAKES 6 SERVINGS, ABOUT 1 ⅓ CUPS EACH.

BBQ Baked Beans & Sausage

Canned beans are convenient, nutritious and a great value. Here we turn navy beans (although you can use just about any variety) into tasty BBQ baked beans with a few simple pantry items. Then we add chicken sausage and collard greens to make an easy, satisfying entree. Serve with coleslaw and cornbread.

½ cup prepared barbecue sauce (*see Notes*)
½ cup water
2 tablespoons tomato paste
1 tablespoon molasses
⅛ teaspoon salt
   Freshly ground pepper to taste
1 tablespoon canola oil
1 medium onion, chopped
4 cups chopped collard greens (about 10 ounces), tough stems removed
9 ounces cooked chicken sausage links (about 3 links), halved lengthwise and sliced
2 15-ounce cans great northern *or* navy beans, rinsed (*see Notes*), *or* 2⅔ cups cooked (*see How to Cook Beans, page 191*)

1. Whisk barbecue sauce, water, tomato paste, molasses, salt and pepper in a medium bowl.

2. Heat oil in a large saucepan over medium heat. Add onion and collard greens and cook, stirring occasionally, until the collards are wilted, 3 to 5 minutes. Add sausage and cook, stirring, until beginning to brown, about 3 minutes more.

3. Reduce heat to medium-low; add beans and the sauce mixture to the pan. Gently stir to combine, cover and cook until heated through, about 3 minutes.

MAKES 4 SERVINGS, ABOUT 1⅓ CUPS EACH.

ACTIVE TIME: 30 minutes

TOTAL: 30 minutes

PER SERVING:

444 calories; 8 g fat (1 g sat, 2 g mono); 45 mg cholesterol; 66 g carbohydrate; 28 g protein; 14 g fiber; 653 mg sodium; 987 mg potassium.

NUTRITION BONUS:

Folate (61% daily value), Vitamin A (50% dv), Vitamin C (35% dv), Magnesium (33% dv), Potassium (28% dv), Iron (24% dv), Calcium (20% dv).

H⬆F H❤H

NOTES:

Check the sodium of your favorite barbecue sauce—some can be quite high. This recipe was developed with a sauce containing 240 mg sodium per 2-tablespoon serving.

Canned beans are convenient but tend to be high in sodium. Give them a good rinse before adding to a recipe to rid them of some of their sodium (up to 35 percent) or opt for low-sodium or no-salt-added varieties. Or, if you have the time, cook your own beans from scratch. You'll find recipes for cooking beans on the stovetop or in a slow cooker on page 191.

Honey-Mustard Turkey Cutlets & Potatoes

For this flavor-packed recipe, potatoes, leeks and lean turkey cutlets are roasted with a honey, mustard and curry sauce. To save a bit on the turkey, you can buy a whole breast or tenderloin and slice your own cutlets. Tightly wrap what you don't use and freeze for up to 3 months. Serve with steamed snow peas and carrots and a glass of white wine.

ACTIVE TIME: 25 minutes

TOTAL: 40 minutes

PER SERVING:

364 calories; 8 g fat (1 g sat, 5 g mono); 70 mg cholesterol; 43 g carbohydrate; 31 g protein; 3 g fiber; 362 mg sodium; 947 mg potassium.

NUTRITION BONUS:

Vitamin C (50% daily value), Potassium (27% dv), Iron (22% dv), Vitamin A (20% dv).

3	medium leeks, white and light green parts only, thinly sliced
1	pound Yukon Gold potatoes, thinly sliced
2	tablespoons canola oil, divided
½	teaspoon freshly ground pepper, divided
¼	teaspoon salt, divided
3	tablespoons honey
3	tablespoons Dijon mustard
1½	teaspoons curry powder
1	pound turkey cutlets

1. Preheat oven to 450°F. Coat a rimmed baking sheet with cooking spray.

2. Place sliced leeks in a colander; rinse and drain well. Toss the leeks, potatoes, 1 tablespoon oil, ¼ teaspoon pepper and ⅛ teaspoon salt on the prepared baking sheet. Bake for 15 minutes, stirring once.

3. Meanwhile, whisk the remaining 1 tablespoon oil, honey, mustard and curry powder in a small bowl until smooth. Sprinkle both sides of turkey with the remaining ¼ teaspoon pepper and ⅛ teaspoon salt.

4. Reduce oven temperature to 400°. Toss the leeks and potatoes with 2 tablespoons of the honey-mustard sauce. Place the turkey on top of the vegetables and spread the remaining sauce over the turkey. Return to the oven and bake until the turkey is cooked through and the potatoes are tender, 12 to 15 minutes more.

MAKES 4 SERVINGS.

ACTIVE TIME: 40 minutes

TOTAL: 50 minutes

PER SERVING:

191 calories; 9 g fat (2 g sat, 4 g mono); 43 mg cholesterol; 11 g carbohydrate; 16 g protein; 2 g fiber; 258 mg sodium; 42 mg potassium.

H✖W H♥H

GRILL VARIATION:

Preheat grill to medium-high. Oil a folded paper towel, hold it with tongs and rub it over the grill rack. (Do not use cooking spray on a hot grill.) Grill the burgers, flipping gently to avoid breaking them, 5 to 6 minutes per side. (An instant-read thermometer inserted in the center should read 165°F.)

Cranberry & Herb Turkey Burgers

Our usual problem with turkey burgers is the dry, chewy texture of the cooked meat. The usual solution is to add fat, but a little sautéed onion, dried cranberries and couscous work just as well. With sage and thyme, call it a summery answer to Thanksgiving dinner. If you like, you can also make this burger with lean ground chicken, beef or even bison.

1/4	cup plus 2 tablespoons whole-wheat couscous
1/2	cup boiling water
2	tablespoons extra-virgin olive oil
1	small onion, finely chopped
1	stalk celery, minced
1	tablespoon chopped fresh thyme *or* 1 teaspoon dried
1 1/2	teaspoons chopped fresh sage *or* 1/2 teaspoon dried, rubbed
1/2	teaspoon salt
1/2	teaspoon freshly ground pepper
1/4	cup dried cranberries, finely chopped
1	pound 93%-lean ground turkey

1. Place couscous in a large bowl. Pour in boiling water, stir and set aside until the water is absorbed, about 5 minutes.

2. Heat oil in a large skillet over medium heat. Add onion and cook, stirring, for 1 minute. Add celery; cook, stirring, until softened, about 3 minutes. Add thyme, sage, salt and pepper; cook until fragrant, about 20 seconds more. Transfer the mixture to the bowl with the couscous, add cranberries and stir to combine. Let cool for 5 minutes. Add turkey and stir until combined; do not overmix. Form the mixture into 6 patties.

3. Coat a large nonstick or cast-iron skillet with cooking spray and set over medium-high heat for 2 minutes. Add the patties, reduce heat to medium, and cook for 4 minutes. Turn and cook on the other side for 2 minutes. Cover and continue to cook until lightly browned but still juicy (the juices should run clear, not pink), about 4 minutes more. (An instant-read thermometer inserted in the center should read 165°F.)

MAKES 6 SERVINGS.

Picadillo-Style Turkey Chili

This chili was inspired by picadillo, a Latin dish typically made with ground meat, tomatoes, spices and sometimes olives and raisins. It's served in pastries, with tortillas or along with rice and beans. Here we decided to make it into a saucy chili. Serve it with crackers or some crusty bread and hot sauce.

ACTIVE TIME: 25 minutes

TOTAL: 35 minutes

TO MAKE AHEAD: Cover and refrigerate for up to 3 days or freeze for up to 3 months.

PER SERVING:

305 calories; 11 g fat (2 g sat, 4 g mono); 43 mg cholesterol; 33 g carbohydrate; 22 g protein; 10 g fiber; 681 mg sodium; 734 mg potassium.

NUTRITION BONUS:

Vitamin A (34% daily value), Vitamin C (32% dv), Iron (26% dv), Potassium (21% dv).

H✖W   H⬆F   H❤H

2	teaspoons plus 1 tablespoon extra-virgin olive oil, divided
1	pound 93%-lean ground turkey
2	medium onions, chopped
4	cloves garlic, minced
2	tablespoons chili powder
1	tablespoon ground cumin
½	teaspoon ground cinnamon
½	teaspoon freshly ground pepper
¼	teaspoon salt
2	cups water
1	28-ounce can crushed tomatoes
1	15-ounce can small red beans, kidney beans *or* pinto beans, rinsed (*see Note, page 199*)
¼	cup sliced green olives, rinsed
¼	cup raisins

1. Heat 2 teaspoons oil in a Dutch oven over medium-high heat. Add turkey and cook, stirring and breaking up with a wooden spoon, until no longer pink, 3 to 4 minutes. Transfer to a plate.

2. Reduce the heat to medium and add the remaining 1 tablespoon oil to the pan. Add onions and garlic and cook, stirring often, until beginning to soften and brown slightly, 5 to 7 minutes. Stir in chili powder, cumin, cinnamon, pepper and salt and cook, stirring, until fragrant, about 30 seconds. Add water, tomatoes, beans, olives, raisins and the turkey; bring to a boil over medium-high heat. Reduce heat to maintain a simmer and cook until the vegetables are soft, 10 to 15 minutes.

MAKES 6 SERVINGS, ABOUT 1 ⅓ CUPS EACH.

Stuffed Tomatoes with Golden Crumb Topping (*page 112*)

BEEF, PORK & LAMB

You can enjoy a steak dinner, a pork tenderloin or a lean leg of lamb for less than a takeout meal if you're savvy. We always keep serving sizes to a healthy 3 ounces of cooked meat—which makes it healthier and more affordable. And obviously ground meat is a great choice when you're on a budget—just remember, you can dress it up as we do with these stuffed tomatoes.

ACTIVE TIME: 30 minutes

TOTAL: 1 hour

PER SERVING:

355 calories; 16 g fat (5 g sat, 7 g mono); 35 mg cholesterol; 33 g carbohydrate; 21 g protein; 6 g fiber; 687 mg sodium; 694 mg potassium.

NUTRITION BONUS:

Vitamin C (90% daily value), Calcium & Vitamin A (25% dv), Potassium & Zinc (20% dv), Magnesium (19% dv), Iron (16% dv).

H✖W   H↑F   H♥H

········SAVE········

Save the scooped-out tomato pulp to use in fresh tomato soup or pasta sauce. It will keep in the refrigerator for up to 3 days or in the freezer for up to 6 months.

Stuffed Tomatoes with Golden Crumb Topping

This comforting dish is a perfect way to take advantage of low-cost ground meat and those big, hothouse tomatoes that aren't quite good enough for salad but will intensify in flavor and sweetness in the oven. For vegetarians, omit the beef or turkey and add beans instead. Serve with a mixed green salad studded with garden-fresh vegetables. (Photograph: page 110.)

4	ounces 90%-lean ground beef *or* 93%-lean ground turkey
1	cup cooked brown rice
4	large ripe but firm tomatoes (about 8 ounces each)
½	teaspoon kosher salt, divided
	Freshly ground pepper to taste
½	cup petite green peas (cooked, if fresh; just thawed, if frozen)
¼	cup minced red onion
½	cup grated Parmigiano-Reggiano cheese, divided
1	tablespoon minced flat-leaf parsley
1	cup fresh whole-wheat breadcrumbs (*see Note, page 198*)
2	tablespoons extra-virgin olive oil
1	small clove garlic, minced

1. Preheat oven to 350°F. Coat an 8-inch-square baking dish with cooking spray.

2. Cook ground beef (or turkey) in a small skillet over medium-high heat, crumbling with a spoon, until brown and cooked through, 1 to 2 minutes. Transfer to a large bowl. Stir in rice.

3. Slice enough off the top of each tomato to remove the core (½ to 1 inch). Scoop out the tomato pulp using a teaspoon or melon baller. Finely chop ½ cup of the pulp and add to the bowl with the meat and rice. (Reserve the remaining pulp for another use, if desired.) Season the inside of the tomatoes with ¼ teaspoon salt and pepper.

4. Add peas, onion, ¼ cup cheese, parsley, the remaining ¼ teaspoon salt and pepper to the meat mixture. Stir to combine. Divide the mixture evenly among the tomatoes and place the tomatoes in the prepared baking dish. Combine the remaining ¼ cup cheese, breadcrumbs, oil and garlic in a small bowl. Sprinkle the mixture on top of the tomatoes.

5. Bake the tomatoes until the crumbs are golden and the tomatoes are soft, 25 to 30 minutes. Serve immediately.

MAKES 4 SERVINGS.

Brown Rice Curried Meatloaf

Meatloaf need not be boring or dry. This version is moist with cooked rice and plenty of vegetables. Curry powder gives extra flavor to the meatloaf and mango chutney spread on top stands in for the traditional ketchup topping. If you have leftover mango chutney try using it in the Curried Red Lentil Soup (page 25).

ACTIVE TIME: 35 minutes

TOTAL: 2 hours

PER SERVING:

342 calories; 14 g fat (4 g sat, 4 g mono); 113 mg cholesterol; 20 g carbohydrate; 33 g protein; 2 g fiber; 586 mg sodium; 558 mg potassium.

NUTRITION BONUS:

Zinc (47% daily value), Iron (21% dv), Potassium (16% dv).

H✷W

½ cup long-grain brown rice
1 cup water
1 medium zucchini, shredded using the large holes of a box grater
1 tablespoon walnut oil *or* extra-virgin olive oil
1 tablespoon minced fresh ginger
2 cloves garlic, minced
1 medium yellow onion, finely chopped
2 stalks celery, finely chopped
1 tablespoon curry powder
2 teaspoons Worcestershire sauce
1 teaspoon salt
2 pounds 93%-lean ground beef
1 large egg, beaten
⅓ cup mango chutney, plus more for serving, if desired

1. Bring rice and water to a boil in a small saucepan over high heat. Reduce heat to low, cover, and simmer at the lowest bubble until the water is absorbed and the rice is tender, 30 to 50 minutes. (You'll need to check after 30 minutes as this is a small batch of rice and may be done by then.) Remove from the heat and let stand, covered, for 10 minutes.

2. Meanwhile, squeeze any excess moisture from zucchini. Heat oil in a large skillet over medium heat. Add ginger and garlic and cook, stirring, until fragrant, 30 seconds. Add onion, celery and the zucchini; cook, stirring often, until softened, about 5 minutes. Stir in curry powder; cook 1 minute. Stir in Worcestershire sauce and salt until combined. Transfer to a large bowl and let cool for 15 minutes.

3. Preheat oven to 350°F. Coat a rimmed baking sheet or broiler pan with cooking spray.

4. Spoon the cooked rice onto a clean cutting board and chop the grains into small bits with a large knife. Transfer to the bowl with the vegetables, add ground beef and egg and gently mix until just combined. Place the mixture on the prepared pan and shape into a loaf, about 10 inches by 5 inches. Spread chutney evenly over the top.

5. Bake until an instant-read thermometer inserted into the center of the meatloaf registers 165°F, 1 hour to 1¼ hours. Let cool for 10 minutes before slicing. Serve with additional mango chutney, if desired.

MAKES 8 SERVINGS.

Portobello & Beef Patty Melt

We made over this diner classic by replacing some of the ground beef with finely chopped portobello mushrooms, which add moisture and flavor but cut the fat and calories. Look for bins of loose mushrooms in your produce section so you can pick the best quality and just the amount you need. We like a smear of pickle relish on top, but you could try chutney, mustard or hot pepper relish in its place. Round out the plate with roasted sweet potatoes and cauliflower.

12	ounces 93%-lean ground beef
2	cups finely chopped portobello mushroom caps (about 2), gills removed (*see Note*)
3	tablespoons plain dry breadcrumbs (*see Note, page 198*)
1	tablespoon Worcestershire sauce
1	teaspoon chopped fresh thyme *or* ½ teaspoon dried
¼	teaspoon salt
¼	teaspoon freshly ground pepper
4	slices rye bread
1	clove garlic, peeled
8	teaspoons pickle relish
4	slices Swiss cheese (2 ounces)

1. Position rack in upper third of oven; preheat broiler. Line a broiler pan with foil.

2. Gently mix beef, mushrooms, breadcrumbs, Worcestershire, thyme, salt and pepper in a medium bowl until combined. Shape into 4 patties and place on the prepared pan. Broil until cooked though, 4 to 6 minutes per side.

3. Meanwhile, toast bread. Rub each slice of toast with garlic.

4. Place 1 patty on each piece of toast, top each with 2 teaspoons relish and cover with a slice of cheese. Remove foil and place the sandwiches on the pan; broil until the cheese is just melted, 30 to 60 seconds.

MAKES 4 SERVINGS.

Beef & Cabbage Stir-Fry with Peanut Sauce

The subtly sweet peanut sauce blends deliciously in this beef, cabbage and carrot stir-fry. Spice up the dish with a few dashes of your favorite hot sauce. Serve with udon noodles or brown rice.

ACTIVE TIME: 40 minutes

TOTAL: 40 minutes

PER SERVING:

364 calories; 17 g fat (3 g sat, 5 g mono); 42 mg cholesterol; 23 g carbohydrate; 31 g protein; 7 g fiber; 469 mg sodium; 866 mg potassium.

NUTRITION BONUS:

Vitamin A (140% daily value), Vitamin C (110% dv), Folate (40% dv), Potassium (25% dv), Magnesium (19% dv).

H✕W   H↑F   H♥H

¼	cup smooth natural peanut butter
⅓	cup orange juice
3	tablespoons reduced-sodium soy sauce
1	tablespoon rice vinegar
2	teaspoons sugar
4	teaspoons canola oil, divided
3	cloves garlic, minced
1	pound sirloin steak, trimmed and thinly sliced (*see Note*)
1	small head Savoy cabbage, thinly sliced
2-5	tablespoons water
2	medium carrots, grated
¼	cup chopped unsalted roasted peanuts (optional)

NOTE:

Freeze beef for 30 minutes to make it easier to cut into very thin slices.

1. Whisk peanut butter, orange juice, soy sauce, vinegar and sugar in a medium bowl until smooth.

2. Heat 2 teaspoons oil in a wok or large skillet over medium-high heat. Add garlic and cook, stirring, until fragrant, 30 seconds. Add steak and cook, stirring, until browned and barely pink in the middle, 2 to 4 minutes. Transfer to a bowl.

3. Reduce heat to medium. Swirl in the remaining 2 teaspoons oil. Add cabbage and 2 tablespoons water; cook, stirring, until beginning to wilt, 3 to 5 minutes. Add carrots (and more water if necessary to prevent sticking or burning) and cook, stirring, until just tender, about 3 minutes more. Return the steak and any accumulated juices to the pan, then pour in the peanut sauce and toss to combine. Serve sprinkled with peanuts (if using).

MAKES 4 SERVINGS.

SAVE

Sirloin is a great choice when it comes to steak because it's lean and relatively inexpensive. In recipes like this one where you slice the beef thinly, you can save even more by substituting budget-priced cuts like eye of round and top round. These leaner cuts have great flavor, but can be tougher, which works fine when you slice them.

ACTIVE TIME: 20 minutes

TOTAL: 6 hours 20 minutes (including 6 hours marinating time)

TO MAKE AHEAD: Prepare through Step 1 up to 1 day in advance.

PER SERVING:

223 calories; 13 g fat (7 g sat, 2 g mono); 65 mg cholesterol; 2 g carbohydrate; 24 g protein; 0 g fiber; 328 mg sodium; 296 mg potassium.

NUTRITION BONUS:

Zinc (28% daily value).

NOTE:

To **oil a grill rack**, oil a folded paper towel and use tongs to rub it over the rack. Do not use cooking spray on a hot grill.

Grilled Steaks Balsamico

A simple marinade of pureed dried figs and store-bought balsamic vinaigrette adds intense flavor to steak. The recipe calls for sirloin steak, which isn't as pricy as strip or tenderloin, but is flavorful and relatively lean. Round steaks are also a good option. Both sirloin and round can be a bit chewier than the more expensive cuts, so be careful not to overcook them. This recipe is adapted from Lori Welander's grand prize–winning recipe from the 2003 National Beef Cook-Off.

> ⅓   cup prepared balsamic vinaigrette
> 2   dried figs, stems trimmed, chopped
> 1   pound sirloin steak, 1 inch thick, trimmed
> ¼   teaspoon salt
>   Freshly ground pepper to taste
> ⅓   cup herb & garlic creamy cheese spread, such as Boursin

1. Place vinaigrette and figs in a blender or food processor; process until blended. Place in a large sealable plastic bag with steak and turn to coat. Marinate in the refrigerator for at least 6 hours or up to 24 hours.

2. Preheat grill to medium.

3. Remove the steak from the marinade; discard marinade. Oil the grill rack (*see Note*). Grill the steak for 4 to 6 minutes per side for medium-rare, depending on thickness. Transfer to a clean cutting board. Season with salt and pepper, tent with foil and let rest for 5 minutes.

4. Meanwhile, warm cheese in a small saucepan over medium-low heat, stirring often, until melted. Carve the steak into thin slices. Serve each portion with a dollop of the cheese sauce.

MAKES 4 SERVINGS.

Oven Barbecued Brisket

In this recipe we use a flavorful rub to give brisket an amazing barbecued flavor in the oven. Like most inexpensive cuts of meat, brisket is priced low for a reason—it's tough. But tough cuts are also usually the most flavorful and just need a little extra time and lovin' to bring out the tenderness. To defeat the toughness, this tasty brisket gets baked using a low and slow cooking method that leaves the meat ready to fall apart. When purchasing a brisket, ask for the leaner flat "first-cut" section, which is a far better choice for healthy eating than the fattier "point cut." It may be worth calling ahead to make sure your supermarket or butcher has one on hand.

ACTIVE TIME: 30 minutes

TOTAL: 12 hours (including 8 hours marinating time)

TO MAKE AHEAD: Bake the brisket, slice and let cool in the sauce for 1 hour; cover with foil and refrigerate for up to 3 days or freeze for up to 1 month. Reheat, covered, in a preheated 350°F oven for 40 minutes; if frozen, defrost in the refrigerator overnight before re-heating.

PER SERVING:

270 calories; 8 g fat (3 g sat, 3 g mono); 78 mg cholesterol; 9 g carbohydrate; 39 g protein; 1 g fiber; 224 mg sodium; 405 mg potassium.

NUTRITION BONUS:

Zinc (61% daily value), Iron (23% dv), Vitamin A (20% dv), Vitamin C (15% dv).

2	medium shallots, minced
2	cloves garlic, minced
4	teaspoons chili powder
4	teaspoons smoked paprika *or* Hungarian paprika (*see Note, page 198*)
2	teaspoons ground cinnamon
2	teaspoons dried oregano
1	teaspoon kosher salt
4	pounds first-cut brisket (*or* flat-cut), trimmed
¼	cup Worcestershire sauce
1	14-ounce can no-salt-added diced tomatoes
¼	cup packed dark brown sugar
¼	cup cider vinegar

1. Combine shallots, garlic, chili powder, paprika, cinnamon, oregano and salt in a small bowl. Rub into both sides of meat. Set the meat in a 9-by-13-inch baking dish, cover and refrigerate for at least 8 hours or overnight.

2. Pour Worcestershire sauce over the meat. Cover the pan with foil and set aside at room temperature while the oven heats to 350°F.

3. Bake the brisket, covered, for 2 hours. Meanwhile, blend tomatoes, brown sugar and vinegar in a blender or food processor until smooth.

4. After 2 hours, pour the tomato mixture over the meat; continue baking, covered, basting with pan juices every 30 minutes, until fork-tender, about 1½ hours more.

5. Remove the meat from the sauce. Let rest for 10 minutes, then slice against the grain. Skim the fat from the sauce in the pan; pour the sauce over the meat and serve (or follow make-ahead instructions).

MAKES 12 SERVINGS.

ACTIVE TIME: 30 minutes

TOTAL: 4½ to 5 hours (slow cooker on high) *or* 7½ to 8 hours (on low)

PREP AHEAD: Trim beef and coat with spice mixture. Prepare vegetables. Combine tomatoes, broth, Worcestershire sauce and garlic. Cover and refrigerate separately for up to 1 day.

TO MAKE AHEAD: Cover and refrigerate for up to 2 days or freeze for up to 4 months.

EQUIPMENT: 4-quart or larger slow cooker

PER SERVING:

177 calories; 5 g fat (2 g sat, 2 g mono); 49 mg cholesterol; 7 g carbohydrate; 25 g protein; 1 g fiber; 340 mg sodium; 288 mg potassium.

NUTRITION BONUS:

Vitamin C (40% daily value), Zinc (38% dv), Vitamin A (25% dv).

H✖W   H♥H

NOTE:

Paprika specifically labeled as "Hungarian" is worth seeking out for this dish because it delivers a fuller, richer flavor than regular or Spanish paprika. Find it at specialty-foods stores or online at *HungarianDeli.com* and *penzeys.com*.

⋯⋯⋯ S A V E ⋯⋯⋯⋯

Look for "family packs" of meat, like the stew meat in this recipe. They're usually less expensive per pound. Refrigerate just what you need, then wrap the rest well and freeze it until you're ready to use it.

Hungarian Beef Goulash

This hearty goulash is a streamlined, slow-cooker version of the traditional Hungarian recipe. Instead of the time-consuming process of browning the beef, the chunks are coated in a spice crust to give a rich mahogany hue. Serve over whole-wheat egg noodles or, for something different, try prepared potato gnocchi or spaetzle.

2	pounds beef stew meat (such as chuck), trimmed and cubed
2	teaspoons caraway seeds
1½-2	tablespoons sweet *or* hot paprika (*or* a mixture of the two), preferably Hungarian (*see Note*)
¼	teaspoon salt
	Freshly ground pepper to taste
1	large *or* 2 medium onions, chopped
1	small red bell pepper, chopped
1	14-ounce can diced tomatoes
1	14-ounce can reduced-sodium beef broth
1	teaspoon Worcestershire sauce
3	cloves garlic, minced
2	bay leaves
1	tablespoon cornstarch mixed with 2 tablespoons water
2	tablespoons chopped fresh parsley

1. Place beef in a 4-quart or larger slow cooker. Crush caraway seeds with the bottom of a saucepan. Transfer to a small bowl and stir in paprika, salt and pepper. Sprinkle the beef with the spice mixture and toss to coat well. Top with onion and bell pepper.

2. Combine tomatoes, broth, Worcestershire sauce and garlic in a medium saucepan; bring to a simmer. Pour over the beef and vegetables. Place bay leaves on top. Cover and cook until the beef is very tender, 4 to 4½ hours on high or 7 to 7½ hours on low.

3. Discard the bay leaves; skim or blot any visible fat from the surface of the stew. Add the cornstarch mixture to the stew, cover and cook on high, stirring 2 or 3 times, until slightly thickened, 10 to 15 minutes. Serve sprinkled with parsley.

MAKES 8 SERVINGS, ABOUT 1 CUP EACH.

Chinese Pork & Vegetable Hot Pot

There is more to Chinese cooking than speedy stir-fries. Richly flavored red braises, cooked in clay pots, make warming winter meals that can be adapted to a slow cooker. Typically, seasonings of anise, cinnamon and ginger distinguish these dishes. Pork shoulder is a cheap cut that starts out tough, but becomes meltingly tender during the slow braise. If you like, you can substitute beef chuck stew meat or even chunked leg of lamb for the pork. Serve over noodles or brown rice, with stir-fried napa cabbage.

2	cups baby carrots
2	medium white turnips (8 ounces total), peeled and cut into ¾-inch-wide wedges
2¼	pounds boneless pork shoulder (picnic *or* Boston-butt), trimmed and cut into 1½-inch chunks
1	bunch scallions, sliced, white and green parts separated
1	14-ounce can reduced-sodium chicken broth
½	cup water
¼	cup reduced-sodium soy sauce
3	tablespoons medium *or* dry sherry (*see Note, page 198*)
4	teaspoons brown sugar
2	tablespoons minced fresh ginger
1	tablespoon rice vinegar
2-4	teaspoons Chinese chile-garlic sauce
4	cloves garlic, minced
1	star anise pod (*see Notes*) *or* 1 teaspoon aniseed
1	cinnamon stick
4	teaspoons cornstarch mixed with 2 tablespoons water
2	tablespoons toasted sesame seeds (*see Notes*) for garnish

1. Place carrots and turnips in the bottom and up the sides of a 4-quart or larger slow cooker. Top with pork and scallion whites. Combine broth, water, soy sauce, sherry, brown sugar, ginger, vinegar, chile-garlic sauce to taste and garlic in a medium saucepan; bring to a simmer over medium-high heat. Pour over the pork and vegetables. Nestle star anise pod (or aniseed) and cinnamon stick into the stew. Cover and cook until the pork and vegetables are tender, 3 to 3½ hours on high or 5½ to 6 hours on low.

2. Discard the star anise pod and cinnamon stick. Skim or blot any visible fat from the surface of the stew. Add the cornstarch mixture to the stew, cover and cook on high, stirring 2 or 3 times, until slightly thickened, 10 to 15 minutes. Serve sprinkled with scallion greens and sesame seeds.

MAKES 6 SERVINGS, 1 GENEROUS CUP EACH.

ACTIVE TIME: 40 minutes

TOTAL: 3 hours 40 minutes to 4 hours 10 minutes (slow cooker on high) or 6 hours 10 minutes to 6 hours 40 minutes (on low)

PREP AHEAD: Trim and cube pork. Prepare vegetables. Combine measured liquids and seasonings. Cover and refrigerate separately for up to 1 day.

TO MAKE AHEAD: Cover and refrigerate for up to 2 days or freeze for up to 4 months.

EQUIPMENT: 4-quart or larger slow cooker

PER SERVING:

390 calories, 22 g fat (8 g sat, 10 g mono); 111 mg cholesterol; 14 g carbohydrate; 32 g protein; 2 g fiber; 537 mg sodium; 573 mg potassium.

NUTRITION BONUS:

Vitamin A (115% daily value), Zinc (40% dv), Vitamin C (25% dv), Iron (17% dv), Potassium (16% dv).

H✳W H♥H

NOTES:

Star anise (named for its star-shaped pods) lends a distinctive licorice-like flavor to numerous Asian dishes. The pods come from a small evergreen tree that is native to China. Look for star anise in the bulk spice sections of natural-foods stores, in Asian markets or online at *penzeys.com.*

Sesame seeds can be purchased already toasted. If you can't find them, toast your own in a small dry skillet over low heat, stirring constantly, until golden and fragrant, about 2 minutes.

ACTIVE TIME: 40 minutes

TOTAL: 2 1/2 hours (plus bean-soaking time)

TO MAKE AHEAD: Cover and refrigerate for up to 3 days.

PER SERVING:

351 calories; 8 g fat (3 g sat, 1 g mono); 45 mg cholesterol; 45 g carbohydrate; 24 g protein; 14 g fiber; 603 mg sodium; 814 mg potassium.

NUTRITION BONUS:

Vitamin C (80% daily value), Folate (63% dv), Potassium (23% dv), Iron & Vitamin A (20% dv).

H✖W   H⬆F   H♥H

NOTES:

Andouille sausage is a smoky, mildly spicy pork sausage commonly used in Cajun cooking. Look for it near other smoked sausages in large supermarkets or specialty-food stores.

Smoked paprika is a spice made from grinding smoke-dried red peppers. It can be used in many types of savory dishes and is available in some large supermarkets with other spices and at *tienda.com*.

To soak beans using a "quick-soak" method: Place beans in a large saucepan with enough cold water to cover them by 2 inches. Bring to a boil. Boil for 2 minutes. Remove from the heat, cover and let stand for 1 hour.

Pinto Bean & Andouille Sausage Stew

Sausage—which is often made from the leftover cuts of meat—and beans are staples in many cuisines because they are cheap, filling and delicious sources of protein. In this adaptation of the Asturian dish fabada, *pinto beans are seasoned with andouille sausage, bacon, tomatoes, onions, peppers and smoked paprika to make a seriously satisfying stew. Fans of spicy beans should use the full amount of minced chile pepper (or more). Serve with brown rice and sour cream.*

1	pound dry pinto beans
1	tablespoon peanut oil *or* canola oil
12	ounces andouille sausage (*see Notes*), diced
3	slices bacon, chopped
2	cups diced onions
2	cloves garlic, smashed and peeled
1	cup diced red bell pepper
1	cup diced green bell pepper
1-3	teaspoons minced chile pepper, such as serrano *or* jalapeño
1	teaspoon smoked paprika (*see Notes*)
4	large ripe plum tomatoes, seeded and diced
8	cups water
1	teaspoon salt
1/4	teaspoon freshly ground pepper
2	teaspoons freshly grated lime zest
	Juice of 1/2 lime

1. Pick over beans to remove any pebbles or broken beans and rinse under cold water. Place in a bowl, cover with 3 inches of cold water and soak for at least 6 hours or overnight. (*Alternatively, use our quick-soak method: see Notes.*)

2. Heat oil in a large heavy casserole or Dutch oven over medium heat. Add sausage and bacon and cook, stirring occasionally, until the bacon is almost crisp, 7 to 10 minutes. Remove with a slotted spoon to a small bowl; set aside in the refrigerator.

3. Add onions and garlic and cook, stirring, over medium heat, until soft and lightly brown, 3 to 5 minutes. Add bell peppers and chile pepper to taste; continue to cook, stirring, until the mixture is soft, about 3 minutes. Stir in paprika. Add tomatoes and cook until they release their juice, about 2 minutes.

4. Drain the beans. Stir the beans and 8 cups water into the pot; bring to a boil. Reduce heat and simmer, uncovered, for 1 hour. Stir in the reserved sausage and bacon along with salt and pepper. Continue simmering, adding a little water if the beans are dry, until the beans are very soft and beginning to break down, about 30 minutes more. Stir in lime zest and juice.

MAKES 8 SERVINGS, ABOUT 1 1/4 CUPS EACH.

Pork Chops au Poivre

Turn your dining room into a French bistro when you dress up pepper-crusted pork chops with a rich, creamy brandy sauce. If your market has a great price (or you just have a hankering) for sirloin steak or either boneless chicken breast or thighs, the substitution for pork is seamless. Serve with roasted sweet potatoes and green beans.

ACTIVE TIME: 20 minutes

TOTAL: 20 minutes

PER SERVING:

299 calories; 15 g fat (4 g sat, 8 g mono); 72 mg cholesterol; 3 g carbohydrate; 22 g protein; 0 g fiber; 342 mg sodium; 319 mg potassium.

H ✴ W

1	teaspoon coarsely ground black pepper
½	teaspoon salt, divided
4	4-ounce boneless pork chops, ½ inch thick, trimmed
3	tablespoons all-purpose flour
2	tablespoons extra-virgin olive oil
1	medium shallot, minced
½	cup brandy
¼	cup reduced-fat sour cream

1. Combine pepper and ¼ teaspoon salt in a small bowl. Pat the mixture onto both sides of each pork chop. Place flour in a shallow dish; dredge each chop in the flour, shaking off any excess (discard any remaining flour).

2. Heat oil in a large skillet over medium-high heat. Add the chops, reduce heat to medium and cook until browned and just cooked through, 2 to 3 minutes per side. Transfer to a plate and tent with foil to keep warm.

3. Reduce heat to medium-low. Add shallot to the pan and cook, stirring, until softened, about 1 minute. Add brandy and cook, stirring and scraping up any browned bits, until most of the liquid has evaporated, 1 to 2 minutes. Remove from the heat; stir in sour cream and the remaining ¼ teaspoon salt. Serve the pork chops with the sauce.

MAKES 4 SERVINGS.

ACTIVE TIME: 10 minutes

TOTAL: 1 hour 20 minutes

TO MAKE AHEAD: Prepare through
Step 1 up to 1 day ahead.

PER SERVING:

203 calories; 11 g fat (3 g sat, 6 g
mono); 64 mg cholesterol; 1 g
carbohydrate; 23 g protein; 0 g fiber;
337 mg sodium; 358 mg potassium.

H✖W   H♥H

Garlic-Roasted Pork

This amazing roast pork loin is rubbed with a Puerto Rican-inspired blend of garlic, oregano and paprika. Serve warm with red beans and rice. Leftovers from this dish make a good sandwich or a great hash when diced with some potatoes and onions and browned in a skillet with a few drops of olive oil.

6   cloves garlic, crushed and peeled
2   tablespoons extra-virgin olive oil
1   tablespoon dried oregano
1   teaspoon paprika
1   teaspoon salt
½   teaspoon freshly ground pepper
1   2-pound boneless pork loin, trimmed

1. Combine garlic, oil, oregano, paprika, salt and pepper in a food processor or blender and puree. Rub pork all over with the seasoning mix and wrap tightly with plastic wrap or place in a large sealable plastic bag. Let marinate in the refrigerator for at least 20 minutes or up to 1 day.

2. Preheat oven to 350°F.

3. Remove the pork from the plastic and place in a shallow roasting pan. Roast, uncovered, until an instant-read thermometer inserted into the center registers 145°F, 50 minutes to 1 hour. Let rest for 10 minutes, then slice and serve.

MAKES 8 SERVINGS.

Almond-Crusted Pork with Honey-Mustard Dipping Sauce

ACTIVE TIME: 25 minutes

TOTAL: 40 minutes

PER SERVING:

299 calories; 7 g fat (1 g sat, 4 g mono); 74 mg cholesterol; 30 g carbohydrate; 29 g protein; 3 g fiber; 487 mg sodium; 562 mg potassium.

NUTRITION BONUS:

Potassium & Zinc (16% daily value).

H✖W   H❤H

Sliced almonds add a delectable, almost-like-fried-chicken crunch to the breading for these tender pieces of pork. We slice the pork thinly to keep the cooking time quick. The resulting pork "fingers" are great dipped in this surprisingly simple honey, soy and mustard sauce. If you have chicken breasts that you want to slice and use, or even chicken tenders (both of which usually run a bit cheaper than pork tenderloin), by all means go for it; the cooking times should be about the same.

1   cup coarse dry breadcrumbs, preferably whole-wheat (*see Note, page 198*)
½   cup sliced almonds
1   teaspoon garlic powder
½   teaspoon kosher salt
¼   teaspoon freshly ground pepper
1   large egg white, beaten
1   pound pork tenderloin, trimmed and cut diagonally into ½-inch-thick slices

DIPPING SAUCE
¼   cup honey
2   tablespoons reduced-sodium soy sauce
2   tablespoons Dijon mustard

1. Preheat oven to 425°F. Set a wire rack on a baking sheet and coat the rack with cooking spray.

2. Pulse breadcrumbs, almonds, garlic powder, salt and pepper in a food processor until the almonds are coarsely chopped. Transfer the mixture to a shallow dish.

3. Place egg white in another shallow dish. Dip both sides of each pork slice in egg white, then evenly coat with the almond mixture. (Discard any remaining egg white and almond mixture.) Place the pork on the prepared rack and coat on both sides with cooking spray.

4. Bake the pork until it is golden brown and no longer pink in the center, 16 to 18 minutes.

5. **To prepare dipping sauce:** Whisk honey, soy sauce and mustard in a small bowl. Serve the pork with the sauce.

MAKES 4 SERVINGS.

ACTIVE TIME: 20 minutes

TOTAL: 20 minutes

PER SERVING:

167 calories; 5 g fat (1 g sat, 2 g mono); 74 mg cholesterol; 6 g carbohydrate; 24 g protein; 0 g fiber; 358 mg sodium; 447 mg potassium.

NUTRITION BONUS:

Zinc (16% daily value).

H✳W H♥H

Maple-Chili Glazed Pork Medallions

Pork tenderloin medallions are quick to prepare and delicious with this maple-chili glaze,. If you find pork loin chops that are less expensive per pound, they are an excellent alternative. Enjoy with corn on the cob.

1	teaspoon chili powder
1/2	teaspoon salt
1/8	teaspoon ground chipotle pepper
1	pound pork tenderloin, trimmed and cut crosswise into 1-inch-thick medallions
2	teaspoons canola oil
1/4	cup apple cider
1	tablespoon maple syrup
1	teaspoon cider vinegar

1. Mix chili powder, salt and ground chipotle in a small bowl. Sprinkle over both sides of pork.

2. Heat oil in a large skillet over medium-high heat. Add the pork and cook until golden, 1 to 2 minutes per side. Add cider, syrup and vinegar to the pan. Bring to a boil, scraping up any browned bits. Reduce the heat to medium and cook, turning the pork occasionally to coat, until the sauce is reduced to a thick glaze, 1 to 3 minutes. Serve the pork drizzled with the glaze.

MAKES 4 SERVINGS.

Middle Eastern Roast Lamb with Tahini Sauce

Inspired by Middle Eastern shawarma sandwiches, this leg of lamb is seasoned with a flavorful spice paste spiked with garlic, cardamom, paprika and cumin. Grill it over indirect heat to approximate the gentle cooking of a rotisserie. Serve the tahini sauce on the side. Leftovers are great tucked into a pita pocket with shredded lettuce and diced tomatoes. Add hummus to the sandwiches if you don't have that much lamb left.

ACTIVE TIME: 45 minutes

TOTAL: 4 ½ hours (including 2 hours marinating time)

EQUIPMENT: Kitchen string

PER SERVING:

257 calories; 14 g fat (3 g sat, 7 g mono); 76 mg cholesterol; 5 g carbohydrate; 27 g protein; 1 g fiber; 551 mg sodium; 377 mg potassium.

NUTRITION BONUS:

Zinc (32% daily value), Iron & Vitamin C (15% dv).

H✳W   H♥H

8	medium cloves garlic, divided	1	4-pound boneless leg of lamb, butterflied and trimmed (*see Notes*)
2½	teaspoons salt, divided		
2	tablespoons extra-virgin olive oil	½	cup lemon juice
1½	teaspoons ground mace	½	cup tahini (*see Notes*)
1	teaspoon ground cardamom	½	cup minced fresh parsley
1	teaspoon paprika	6	tablespoons nonfat plain yogurt, preferably Greek-style (*see Note, page 199*)
1	teaspoon ground cinnamon		
1	teaspoon ground cumin	¼	cup water
½	teaspoon cayenne pepper	½	teaspoon freshly ground pepper

1. Mince 6 garlic cloves. Place in a small bowl with 1½ teaspoons salt and mash into a paste using the back of a spoon. Stir in oil, mace, cardamom, paprika, cinnamon, cumin and cayenne until combined.

2. Open lamb so it's flat, with the cut side up. Spread three-quarters of the spice paste over the cut surface. Roll the lamb closed and tie in several places so it is about the shape of a large football. Spread the remaining paste over the outside. Loosely cover with plastic wrap and refrigerate for 2 hours.

3. Mince the remaining 2 garlic cloves. Combine with the remaining 1 teaspoon salt in a medium bowl with lemon juice, tahini, parsley, yogurt, water and pepper. Refrigerate until ready to serve.

4. About 20 minutes before you are ready to grill, preheat a gas grill (with all burners lit) to 400°F or build a fire in a charcoal grill and let it burn down to medium heat (about 400°F).

5. If using a gas grill, turn off one burner (leaving 1 to 2 burners lit, depending on your grill). If using a charcoal grill, move the coals to one side. Place the lamb on the unheated side of the rack. Close the lid and roast undisturbed for 30 minutes.

6. Rotate the lamb 180 degrees, cover and continue roasting until an instant-read thermometer inserted into the thickest part of the meat registers 140°F (for medium-rare) to 145° (for medium), 20 to 40 minutes more. Transfer to a clean cutting board; let stand for 10 minutes before slicing. Serve with the tahini sauce.

MAKES 12 SERVINGS.

NOTES:

Have your butcher "butterfly" a boneless **leg of lamb** (that is, open it up to a large, flat cut of meat); ask that any visible fat be trimmed off.

Tahini is a thick paste of ground sesame seeds. Look for it in large supermarkets in the Middle Eastern section or near other nut butters. Store in the refrigerator for up to 6 months.

⋯ **SAVE** ⋯⋯⋯⋯⋯⋯⋯

If you have leftover tahini, try making your own hummus. Puree in a food processor: one 16-ounce can of chickpeas, ⅓ cup tahini, 3 to 4 tablespoons lemon juice and 2 to 3 tablespoons water, 1 minced garlic clove, and salt & pepper to taste.

Louisiana Catfish with Okra & Corn (*page 138*)

FISH & SEAFOOD

6

Doctors recommend eating fish or seafood twice a week, especially fish rich in omega-3s, such as salmon and tuna. If you're looking to save money, try our recipes for canned tuna and canned wild salmon as well as sustainably fished or farmed shrimp, tilapia, catfish and trout.

ACTIVE TIME: 30 minutes

TOTAL: 30 minutes

PER SERVING:

288 calories; 15 g fat (3 g sat, 9 g mono); 53 mg cholesterol; 19 g carbohydrate; 21 g protein; 4 g fiber; 311 mg sodium; 695 mg potassium.

NUTRITION BONUS:

Vitamin C (30% daily value), Folate & Potassium (20% dv), Magnesium (19% dv).

H✕W   H♥H

NOTE:

The catfish-farming industry has grown in the U.S. and the quality of the fish has improved. Farmers raise **catfish** sustainably in closed pens and feed them a mostly vegetarian diet. If you're wary of fish but enjoy bold flavors, this is a good recipe to help you get more heart-healthy fish into your diet.

SAVE

Premixed seasoning blends offer complex flavors without having to buy lots of separate spices. In this 30-minute dinner, Cajun or Creole seasoning flavors both the catfish and the vegetables. You can also use it to liven up plain popcorn, toss it with roasted nuts or sprinkle it on oven fries.

Louisiana Catfish with Okra & Corn

This dish is best with fresh vegetables, but we were pleasantly surprised at how well it turned out with economical frozen okra and corn. Serve with cheese grits and a green salad. (Photograph: page 136.)

2	cups fresh *or* frozen sliced okra
1 ¾	cups fresh corn kernels (from 2 ears; *see Note, page 200*) *or* frozen
1	medium onion, diced
2	teaspoons plus 1 tablespoon extra-virgin olive oil, divided
1 ¾	teaspoons Cajun *or* Creole seasoning, divided
1	pound U.S. farmed catfish fillets (*see Note*), patted dry and cut into 4 portions

1. Preheat oven to 450°F.

2. Combine okra, corn, onion, 2 teaspoons oil and ¾ teaspoon Cajun (or Creole) seasoning in a large bowl. Spread the mixture out on a large rimmed baking sheet. Roast, stirring twice, until the vegetables are tender and beginning to brown, 20 to 25 minutes.

3. Meanwhile, sprinkle both sides of catfish with the remaining 1 teaspoon seasoning. Heat the remaining 1 tablespoon oil in a large nonstick skillet over medium-high heat. Reduce heat to medium, add the fish and cook until just cooked through and starting to brown, about 4 minutes per side. Serve with the roasted vegetables.

MAKES 4 SERVINGS.

Pan-Fried Trout

Marinating stronger-flavored fish like trout in buttermilk eliminates some of the fishy flavors. A quick turn in cornmeal makes a crunchy, crusty exterior.

ACTIVE TIME: 30 minutes

TOTAL: 1 hour

PER SERVING:

275 calories; 12 g fat (3 g sat, 5 g mono); 84 mg cholesterol, 10 g carbohydrate; 31 g protein; 1 g fiber; 362 mg sodium; 703 mg potassium.

NUTRITION BONUS:

Potassium (20% daily value), Magnesium (15% dv), source of omega-3s.

H✈W   H♥H

NOTE:

You can buy trout with the bones and heads removed (easier than cleaning them yourself); for this recipe, each cleaned trout should weigh about 5 ounces.

⅓	cup nonfat *or* low-fat buttermilk (*see Note, page 199*)
½	teaspoon salt, divided
½	teaspoon freshly ground pepper, divided
4	cleaned whole rainbow trout (about 5 ounces each; *see Note*)
½	cup yellow cornmeal, preferably stone-ground
1-2	tablespoons extra-virgin olive oil, divided
	Lemon wedges

1. Mix buttermilk and ¼ teaspoon each of salt and pepper in a shallow pan or bowl large enough to hold the fish in a single layer. Add fish and turn to coat evenly, rubbing buttermilk into the cavities. Cover and refrigerate for 30 minutes.

2. Put cornmeal in a shallow pan or on a large plate. Shake off the excess buttermilk and sprinkle the fish flesh with the remaining ¼ teaspoon each salt and pepper. Dredge the trout in the cornmeal, turning to coat evenly.

3. Heat 1 tablespoon oil in a large nonstick pan over medium heat. Gently place the fish in the pan. (If your pan is too small to fit all 4 fish, heat 1 tablespoon oil in a second nonstick skillet and cook 2 fish in each pan.) Reduce heat to low and cook the fish until the cornmeal crust is well browned, about 10 minutes. Turn carefully, using tongs or 2 spatulas if needed; continue cooking on the second side until well browned, another 10 minutes. Serve immediately, with lemon wedges.

MAKES 4 SERVINGS.

ACTIVE TIME: 30 minutes

TOTAL: 30 minutes

PER SERVING:

232 calories; 10 g fat (1 g sat, 5 g mono); 168 mg cholesterol; 12 g carbohydrate; 21 g protein; 1 g fiber; 488 mg sodium; 327 mg potassium.

NUTRITION BONUS:

Vitamin C (43% daily value), Iron (20% dv).

H〉〈W   H♥H

NOTES:

Both wild-caught and farm-raised shrimp can damage the surrounding ecosystems when not managed properly. Fortunately, it is possible to buy shrimp that have been raised or caught with sound environmental practices. Look for fresh or frozen shrimp certified by an independent agency, such as Wild American Shrimp or Marine Stewardship Council. If you can't find certified shrimp, choose wild-caught shrimp from North America—it's more likely to be sustainably caught.

Sherry is a type of fortified wine originally from southern Spain. Don't use the "cooking sherry" sold in many supermarkets—it can be surprisingly high in sodium. Instead, get dry sherry that's sold with other fortified wines at your wine or liquor store.

Sesame-Orange Shrimp

These shrimp are super-easy to make—just coat them in a simple batter, cook them in a little oil and toss with a tangy sesame-orange sauce. The staff at EATINGWELL simply could not get enough of these delicious shrimp while we were developing this recipe. Serve with brown rice and steamed snow peas tossed with a little toasted sesame oil.

3	tablespoons sesame seeds (white, black *or* a mix)
2	large egg whites
¼	cup cornstarch
¼	teaspoon salt
¼	teaspoon freshly ground pepper
1	pound raw U.S. shrimp (21-25 per pound; *see Notes*), peeled and deveined
2	tablespoons canola oil, divided
¾	cup orange juice
¼	cup dry sherry (*see Notes*)
2	tablespoons reduced-sodium soy sauce
1	teaspoon sugar
1	scallion, thinly sliced

1. Whisk sesame seeds, egg whites, cornstarch, salt and pepper in a large bowl. Add shrimp and toss to coat.

2. Heat 1 tablespoon oil in a large nonstick skillet over medium heat. Add half the shrimp and cook until golden, 1 to 2 minutes per side. Transfer to a paper towel-lined plate to drain. Repeat with the remaining 1 tablespoon oil and the rest of the shrimp; transfer to the plate.

3. Add orange juice, sherry, soy sauce and sugar to the pan. Bring to a boil and cook, stirring occasionally, until slightly thickened and reduced by half, 4 to 6 minutes. Return the shrimp to the pan and stir to coat with the sauce. Serve immediately, with scallion sprinkled on top.

MAKES 4 SERVINGS.

Grilled Shrimp with Melon & Pineapple Salsa

Grilled shrimp is perfectly accented by this light, summery pineapple-melon salsa. The flavors are bright and fresh, just right for a hot day. Fruit is the best value when it's in season and for this versatile salsa, you can use just one type of melon (even watermelon) or any combination of melons that you find at the market. For best flavor marinate the shrimp overnight. Dice the leftover melon and pineapple for a healthy snack.

1	pound U.S. raw shrimp (16-20 per pound; *see Note, page 200*), peeled and deveined
2	tablespoons canola oil, divided
2	teaspoons finely grated fresh ginger, divided
2	teaspoons minced seeded jalapeño, divided
2	cups finely diced firm ripe melon
1	cup finely diced fresh pineapple
¼	cup finely diced red bell pepper
¼	cup finely diced green bell pepper
¼	cup finely diced red onion
3	tablespoons rice vinegar
2	tablespoons finely chopped fresh mint, plus 4 sprigs for garnish
½	teaspoon kosher salt
4	large lettuce leaves, such as Boston, romaine *or* iceberg
4	lime wedges

1. Combine shrimp, 1 tablespoon oil, 1 teaspoon ginger and 1 teaspoon jalapeño in a medium bowl. Cover and refrigerate for 4 hours or up to 24 hours.

2. Combine melon, pineapple, red and green bell pepper, onion, vinegar, chopped mint and salt in a large bowl with the remaining 1 tablespoon oil, 1 teaspoon ginger and 1 teaspoon jalapeño. Refrigerate until cold, about 30 minutes or up to 4 hours.

3. About 20 minutes before serving, preheat grill to high.

4. Thread the shrimp onto skewers, piercing each twice, once through the tail end and once near the head end. Grill the shrimp until pink and just cooked through, 2 to 3 minutes per side. When cool enough to handle, slide the shrimp off the skewers.

5. To serve, arrange one large lettuce leaf on each dinner plate. Spoon salsa onto the lettuce and top with shrimp. Garnish each serving with a lime wedge and a mint sprig, if using.

MAKES 4 SERVINGS.

ACTIVE TIME: 45 minutes

TOTAL: 1 ¼ hours (plus marinating time)

TO MAKE AHEAD: Marinate the shrimp (Step 1) for up to 24 hours. Cover and refrigerate the salsa (Step 2) for up to 4 hours.

EQUIPMENT: Four 8- to 10-inch skewers

PER SERVING:

211 calories; 8 g fat (1 g sat, 5 g mono); 168 mg cholesterol; 16 g carbohydrate; 19 g protein; 2 g fiber; 352 mg sodium; 501 mg potassium.

NUTRITION BONUS:

Vitamin C (97% daily value), Vitamin A (24% dv), Iron (20% dv).

H✳W H♥H

···SAVE···························

To save money, purchase shrimp with their shells on, then peel and devein them yourself. To peel shrimp, grasp the legs and hold onto the tail while you twist off the shell. The "vein" running along a shrimp's back (technically the dorsal surface, opposite the legs) under a thin layer of flesh is really its digestive tract. To devein shrimp, use a paring knife to make a slit along the length of the shrimp. Under running water, remove the black digestive tract with the knife tip.

ACTIVE TIME: 30 minutes

TOTAL: 30 minutes

PER SERVING:

302 calories; 10 g fat (4 g sat, 3 g mono); 82 mg cholesterol; 29 g carbohydrate; 24 g protein; 3 g fiber; 786 mg sodium; 122 mg potassium.

NUTRITION BONUS:

Vitamin C (57% daily value), Calcium (31% dv), Vitamin A (27% dv), Iron (26% dv).

H✷W   H♥H

NOTE:

Purchase **crabmeat** canned, frozen or pasteurized. The pasteurized usually has the best flavor (it is heated to a lower temperature than canned); look for it in the fresh seafood section of the market. Once opened, the crabmeat should be used within 4 days.

········ SAVE ······················

Citrus zest, the outer peel of citrus fruit, is a healthy way to punch up the flavor in a dish. The best way to get the zest is to rub the fruit on a microplane grater. After zesting, squeeze the juice and re-frigerate or freeze to use in salad dressings or sauces.

Crab Quesadillas

These quesadillas have an irresistibly creamy filling. They also make great appetizers. You don't need the priciest lump crabmeat for this recipe. In a pinch, you can even use imitation crab—just look for one made from Alaskan pollock, which is certified sustainable by the Marine Stewardship Council. Serve with your favorite salsa on top and a cup of black bean soup topped with chopped avocado.

1	cup shredded reduced-fat Cheddar cheese
2	ounces reduced-fat cream cheese, softened
4	scallions, chopped
1/2	medium red bell pepper, finely chopped
1/3	cup chopped fresh cilantro
2	tablespoons chopped pickled jalapeños (optional)
1	teaspoon freshly grated orange zest
1	tablespoon orange juice
8	ounces pasteurized crabmeat, drained and shells removed if necessary (*see Note*)
4	8-inch whole-wheat tortillas
2	teaspoons canola oil, divided

1. Combine Cheddar, cream cheese, scallions, bell pepper, cilantro, jalapeños (if using), orange zest and juice in a medium bowl. Gently stir in crab. Lay tortillas out on a work surface. Spread one-fourth of the filling on half of each tortilla. Fold tortillas in half, pressing gently to flatten.

2. Heat 1 teaspoon oil in a large nonstick skillet over medium heat. Place 2 quesadillas in the pan and cook, turning once, until golden on both sides, 3 to 4 minutes total. Transfer to a cutting board and tent with foil to keep warm. Repeat with the remaining 1 teaspoon oil and quesadillas. To serve, cut each quesadilla into 4 wedges.

MAKES 4 SERVINGS.

Tilapia & Poblano Tacos

Here's a quick take on fish tacos: just sauté fish, onions and peppers and serve with tortillas and some simple toppings. Poblano peppers vary immensely in heat level and tasting them is the only way to judge how hot they are. So before cooking, taste your poblanos and add a pinch of cayenne or a jalapeño if you want more heat. Use green bell peppers if you want a milder taco.

3 teaspoons extra-virgin olive oil, divided
1 pound U.S. farmed tilapia fillets
2 cups diced poblano peppers (about 2 large)
1 medium onion, diced
1 jalapeño pepper, minced (optional)
1 cup fresh corn kernels (from 1 large ear; *see Note, page 200*) *or* frozen (thawed)
2 tablespoons lime juice
1 tablespoon ground cumin
1 teaspoon dried oregano
¾ teaspoon salt
12 6-inch corn tortillas
1 avocado, cubed
¾ cup prepared salsa, preferably green
¼ cup chopped cilantro for garnish

1. Heat 2 teaspoons oil in a large nonstick skillet over medium-high heat. Add tilapia and cook until opaque in the center, 2 to 3 minutes per side. Transfer to a plate and flake with 2 forks.

2. Add the remaining 1 teaspoon oil to the pan and reduce heat to medium. Add poblanos, onion and jalapeño (if using) and cook, stirring often, until softened and starting to brown, 4 to 6 minutes. Stir in corn, lime juice, cumin, oregano and salt. Cook, stirring often, until heated through, 1 to 2 minutes. Stir in the fish and any accumulated juice from the plate.

3. Wrap tortillas in paper towels and heat in the microwave on High until warm and pliable, 30 seconds to 1 minute. Fill each tortilla with about ⅓ cup of the tilapia mixture and top with avocado, salsa and cilantro (if desired).

MAKES 6 SERVINGS, 2 TACOS EACH.

ACTIVE TIME: 35 minutes

TOTAL: 35 minutes

PER SERVING:

345 calories; 11 g fat (2 g sat, 6 g mono); 38 mg cholesterol; 43 g carbohydrate; 20 g protein; 7 g fiber; 590 mg sodium; 608 mg potassium.

NUTRITION BONUS:

Vitamin C (47% daily value), Potassium (17% dv), Folate (16% dv).

H✖W   H⬆F   H♥H

····SAVE·····

U.S. farmed tilapia is a great choice both for the environment and your budget. Plus its mild flavor and relatively firm texture make it super-versatile—try it in other recipes to replace more expensive fish like flounder, sole or cod.

Bean & Salmon Salad with Anchovy-Arugula Dressing

This simple bean-and-salmon salad becomes something truly exciting when dressed with a bold dressing flavored with anchovies and arugula. Canned wild Alaskan salmon is a healthy, economical and environmentally sound choice.

1 ½ cups baby arugula
⅓ cup fresh parsley leaves
¼ cup lemon juice
3 cloves garlic, minced
2 oil-packed anchovy fillets, finely chopped
1 tablespoon chopped shallot
Pinch of salt, plus ¼ teaspoon, divided
¼ cup extra-virgin olive oil
4 cups cooked cannellini beans (*see How to Cook Beans, page 191*), well drained, at room temperature *or* warm, *or* rinsed canned beans
1 6- to 7-ounce can boneless, skinless wild Alaskan salmon (*see Notes*), drained and flaked
¾ cup thinly sliced radishes
1 stalk celery, sliced diagonally ¼ inch thick
Freshly ground pepper to taste
4 large leaves butterhead *or* Boston lettuce
1 avocado, sliced, for garnish

1. Place arugula, parsley, lemon juice, garlic, anchovies, shallot and pinch of salt in a food processor; process until finely chopped. With the motor running, slowly drizzle in oil.

2. Gently combine beans, salmon, radishes, celery, the remaining ¼ teaspoon salt and pepper in a large bowl. Pour in the dressing and gently toss to combine.

3. To serve, line 4 plates with lettuce leaves. Divide the salad evenly among the plates. Garnish with avocado slices, if desired.

MAKES 4 SERVINGS, ABOUT 1 ½ CUPS EACH.

ACTIVE TIME: 30 minutes

TOTAL: 30 minutes

PER SERVING:

415 calories; 16 g fat (2 g sat, 11 g mono), 13 mg cholesterol, 46 g carbohydrate; 25 g protein; 14 g fiber; 516 mg sodium; 935 mg potassium.

NUTRITION BONUS:

Folate (67% daily value), Vitamin C (38% dv), Iron (37% dv), Potassium (27% dv), Magnesium (26% dv), Vitamin A (24% dv), Zinc (16% dv).

H✂W   H⬆F   H❤H

NOTES:

Unless specified, **canned salmon** includes the skin and small bones. Although both are edible, we recommend buying boneless, skinless salmon (labeled as such) for convenience.

Wild-caught salmon from Alaska is the best choice for the environment, according to Monterey Bay Aquarium's Seafood Watch program (visit *seafoodwatch.org* for more information). Farmed salmon, including Atlantic, should be avoided, as it endangers the wild salmon population. Both wild-caught red salmon, also called sockeye, and pink salmon are available in cans. Red salmon has a richer color and meatier texture, while pink salmon is paler and more tender. Look for "wild Alaskan" on the label

ACTIVE TIME: 30 minutes

TOTAL: 30 minutes

PER SERVING:

317 calories; 18 g fat (5 g sat, 7 g mono); 143 mg cholesterol; 19 g carbohydrate; 21 g protein; 2 g fiber; 559 mg sodium; 605 mg potassium.

NUTRITION BONUS:

Potassium (17% daily value), Vitamin C (15% dv), source of omega-3s.

H✳W H♥H

NOTES:

Unless specified, **canned salmon** includes the skin and small bones. Although both are edible, we recommend buying boneless, skinless salmon (labeled as such) for convenience.

Wild-caught salmon from Alaska is the best choice for the environment, according to Monterey Bay Aquarium's Seafood Watch program (visit *seafoodwatch.org* for more information). Farmed salmon, including Atlantic, should be avoided, as it endangers the wild salmon population. Both wild-caught red salmon, also called sockeye, and pink salmon are available in cans. Red salmon has a richer color and meatier texture, while pink salmon is paler and more tender. Look for "wild Alaskan" on the label.

Salmon Rösti

Convenient frozen hash browns and flaked salmon come together for a twist on the traditional Swiss favorite. We love the creamy dill sauce, but a dollop of ketchup is tasty too. Serve with steamed green beans tossed with sliced scallions, Dijon mustard and lemon.

2   6- to 7-ounce cans boneless, skinless wild Alaskan salmon (*see Notes*), drained
½   cup finely chopped red onion
2   large eggs plus 1 large egg white, lightly beaten
1   tablespoon whole-grain mustard
3   tablespoons chopped fresh dill *or* 3 teaspoons dried, divided
½   teaspoon freshly ground pepper
¼   teaspoon salt
4   cups frozen hash-brown shredded potatoes (about 12 ounces)
2   tablespoons extra-virgin olive oil, divided
⅓   cup reduced-fat sour cream
1   tablespoon capers, rinsed and chopped
1   teaspoon lemon juice

1. Combine salmon, onion, eggs and egg white, mustard, 2 tablespoons fresh dill (or 2 teaspoons dried), pepper and salt in a large bowl. Add potatoes and stir to combine.

2. Preheat oven to 200°F.

3. Heat 1 tablespoon oil in a large nonstick skillet over medium heat until shimmering. Fill a 1-cup measure two-thirds full with the salmon mixture and firmly pack it down. Unmold into the pan and pat to form a 3-inch cake. Repeat, making 3 more cakes. Cover and cook until browned on the bottom, 3 to 5 minutes. Gently turn over and cook, covered, until crispy on the other side, 3 to 5 minutes more. Transfer the cakes to a baking dish; keep warm in the oven. Wipe out the skillet and cook 4 more cakes with the remaining 1 tablespoon oil and the remaining salmon mixture.

4. Combine sour cream, capers, lemon juice and the remaining dill in a small bowl. Serve the salmon cakes with the dill sauce.

MAKES 4 SERVINGS, 2 RÖSTI EACH.

ACTIVE TIME: 40 minutes

TOTAL: 40 minutes

PER SERVING:

142 calories; 7 g fat (2 g sat, 4 g
mono); 165 mg cholesterol; 8 g
carbohydrate; 13 g protein; 2 g fiber;
515 mg sodium; 221 mg potassium.

NUTRITION BONUS:

Vitamin C (19% daily value).

H❌W   H♥H

Tortilla with Tuna & Onions

 This thin, Spanish-style omelet uses inexpensive and convenient canned tomatoes and tuna, both of which have all the nutritional benefits of fresh. The tomatoes are loaded with vitamin C and lycopene and the tuna is a good source of omega-3s, which help in the fight against "bad" LDL cholesterol.

2½   teaspoons extra-virgin olive oil, divided
 2   onions, thinly sliced
½   teaspoon salt, divided
½   cup chopped fresh *or* drained canned tomatoes
     Freshly ground pepper to taste
 3   large eggs
 2   large egg whites
 1   5- to 6-ounce can water-packed chunk light tuna, drained and flaked

1. Heat 1½ teaspoons oil in a medium nonstick skillet over medium-low heat. Add onions and ¼ teaspoon salt. Cook, stirring often, until very tender and starting to turn light golden, 10 to 20 minutes. (Add 1 to 2 tablespoons water, if onions are browning too quickly.) Add tomatoes and cook, stirring occasionally, until tomatoes have melted into the onions, about 10 minutes. Season with pepper; set aside to cool.

2. Whisk eggs, egg whites and the remaining ¼ teaspoon salt in a bowl. Fold in tuna and the reserved onion mixture.

3. Wash and dry the pan. Brush the pan with the remaining 1 teaspoon oil. Place over low heat. Add the egg mixture and stir gently to distribute tuna and onions. Cook, moving the pan around on the burner to ensure even cooking, until the underside is golden and the top is starting to set, about 5 minutes. Use a spatula to loosen the tortilla. Invert a large platter over the pan, grasp the platter and pan with oven mitts and carefully turn over. Lift off the pan, slide the tortilla back into it and cook until the bottom is set, about 1 minute. Slide onto a serving platter and cut into wedges. Serve hot or at room temperature.

MAKES 4 SERVINGS.

Calamari, Red Pepper & Lemon Stir-Fry

Once the ingredients are cleaned and chopped, this dish takes under 10 minutes to prepare. Serve with whole-wheat orzo or brown rice.

- 1 pound cleaned calamari (*see Note*)
- 1 small lemon
- 2 tablespoons extra-virgin olive oil, divided
- 1 large red bell pepper, cut into ¾-inch squares, divided
- ⅛ teaspoon crushed red pepper, divided
- ¼ teaspoon salt
- ¼ teaspoon freshly ground pepper
- 3 tablespoons chopped fresh cilantro

1. Slice calamari bodies into ½-inch-thick rings; leave tentacles whole. Rinse carefully inside and out and pat dry. Scrub lemon and cut crosswise into ⅛-inch-thick slices. Cut each slice into quarters and remove any seeds.

2. Heat 1 tablespoon oil in a large heavy skillet over medium-high heat. Add half the bell pepper and half the crushed red pepper; cook, stirring, until barely tender, 1 to 2 minutes. Add half the calamari and cook, stirring, until opaque, 30 to 45 seconds. Add half the lemon pieces and cook, stirring, until the lemon is just heated through, about 30 seconds more. Transfer the mixture to a serving dish and keep warm. Repeat with the remaining ingredients. Season with salt and pepper. Sprinkle with cilantro and serve immediately.

MAKES 4 SERVINGS, ABOUT ¾ CUP EACH.

ACTIVE TIME: 25 minutes

TOTAL: 25 minutes

PER SERVING:

186 calories; 9 g fat (1 g sat, 6 g mono); 264 mg cholesterol; 9 g carbohydrate; 18 g protein; 2 g fiber; 198 mg sodium; 406 mg potassium.

NUTRITION BONUS:

Vitamin C (131% daily value), Vitamin A (27% dv).

H✂W   H♥H

NOTE:

Calamari, also known as squid, is sold frozen or fresh in the seafood department of the grocery store. Look for cleaned calamari, with its cartilage and ink removed; otherwise ask at the fish counter to have it cleaned.

Sesame-Orange flavoring on steamed broccoli and cauliflower (*page 163*)

ON THE SIDE 7

You can keep sides quick and simple but still pack them with flavor if you stock up on spices and flavored oils like the toasted sesame oil used on steamed broccoli and cauliflower in this picture.

APPETIZERS

Slow-Roasted Cherry Tomato Bruschetta

H✂w H♥H

Toss 3 pints **cherry tomatoes** with 1 tablespoon extra-virgin **olive oil**, 3 cloves minced **garlic** and ½ teaspoon each **salt** and freshly ground **pepper**. Roast on a baking sheet at 325°F until broken down, 45 to 55 minutes. Combine roasted tomatoes with ¼ cup sliced fresh **basil** and 1 tablespoon **red-wine vinegar**. Top slices of toasted **baguette** (preferably whole-wheat) with the tomato mixture. Garnish with **anchovy fillets**, **kalamata olives** *or* sliced fresh **basil**.

MAKES 14 SERVINGS.

PER SERVING: 69 calories; 1 g fat (0 g sat, 1 g mono); 0 mg cholesterol; 13 g carbohydrate; 3 g protein; 3 g fiber; 178 mg sodium, 156 mg potassium. **NUTRITION BONUS:** Vitamin C (15% daily value).

Beet Carpaccio

H✂w H⬆F H♥H

Steam 3 red *and/or* golden **beets** (*see page 162*). Peel the beets when cool enough to handle. Slice as thinly as possible, using a mandoline or sharp knife. Arrange the beet slices on a large platter or on 6 salad plates. Sprinkle with ¼ cup crumbled **blue cheese**, 1 teaspoon chopped fresh **herbs**, such as dill, savory *or* tarragon, ¼ teaspoon **salt** and freshly ground **pepper** to taste; drizzle with 2 teaspoons extra-virgin **olive oil**. Serve with slices of toasted *or* grilled **whole-grain baguette** brushed with **olive oil**.

MAKES 6 SERVINGS.

PER SERVING: 132 calories; 5 g fat (1 g sat, 3 g mono); 4 mg cholesterol; 19 g carbohydrate; 5 g protein; 4 g fiber; 330 mg sodium; 177 mg potassium. **NUTRITION BONUS:** Folate (15% daily value).

Tomato-Basil Skewers

H✂w

Thread 16 small fresh **mozzarella balls**, 16 fresh **basil** leaves and 16 **cherry tomatoes** on small skewers. Drizzle with extra-virgin **olive oil** and sprinkle with **coarse salt** and freshly ground **pepper**.

MAKES 16 SKEWERS.

PER SKEWER: 80 calories; 5 g fat (3 g sat, 1 g mono); 19 mg cholesterol; 2 g carbohydrate; 7 g protein; 0 g fiber; 191 mg sodium; 67 mg potassium. **NUTRITION BONUS:** Calcium (24% daily value).

Slow-Roasted Cherry Tomato Bruschetta

Beet Carpaccio

Tomato-Basil Skewers

EatingWell Deviled Eggs

Hard-boil 12 large **eggs** (*see Note, page 199*). Peel the eggs when cool enough to handle. Halve lengthwise with a sharp knife. Gently remove the yolks. Place 16 yolk halves in a food processor (discard the remaining 8 yolk halves or save to put on a salad). Add ⅓ cup nonfat **cottage cheese**, ¼ cup low-fat **mayonnaise**, 3 tablespoons minced fresh **chives** (*or* scallion greens), 1 tablespoon **sweet pickle relish**, 2 teaspoons yellow **mustard** and ⅛ teaspoon **salt**; process until smooth. Spoon about 2 teaspoons of the yolk mixture into each egg white half. Sprinkle with **paprika**, if desired.

MAKES 24 SERVINGS.

PER SERVING: 34 calories; 2 g fat (1 g sat, 1 g mono); 71 mg cholesterol; 1 g carbohydrate; 3 g protein; 0 g fiber; 85 mg sodium; 31 mg potassium.

EatingWell Deviled Eggs

Shrimp Crostini

H✖W   H♥H

Combine ½ cup low-fat **mayonnaise**, 2 tablespoons finely chopped **shallot**, 1 tablespoon finely chopped fresh **parsley**, 1 teaspoon **Dijon mustard** and ½ teaspoon chopped **capers** in a small bowl; cover and refrigerate for at least 15 minutes (or up to 1 day) to blend flavors. Spread 1 teaspoon on each of 16 slices of thin rye (*or* pumpernickel) **cocktail-size bread**. Top each piece with a few cooked salad (*or* baby) **shrimp** and a paper-thin wedge of **lemon**.

MAKES 8 SERVINGS, 2 PIECES EACH.

PER SERVING: 103 calories; 2 g fat (0 g sat, 0 g mono); 48 mg cholesterol; 13 g carbohydrate; 9 g protein; 1 g fiber; 304 mg sodium; 73 mg potassium.

Tuna-Caper Spread

Drain one 5- to 6-ounce can water-packed **chunk light tuna**. Combine the tuna, 4 ounces reduced-fat **cream cheese**, 1 tablespoon extra-virgin **olive oil**, 2 teaspoons lemon juice and ⅛ teaspoon **cayenne pepper**, or more to taste, in a food processor and process until smooth. Transfer to a serving bowl; stir in 3 tablespoons rinsed and chopped **capers**, 2 tablespoons chopped fresh **parsley** and 1½ teaspoons chopped fresh **thyme** (*or* ½ teaspoon dried).

MAKES ABOUT 1 CUP.

PER TABLESPOON: 33 calories; 3 g fat (1 g sat, 1 g mono); 7 mg cholesterol; 0 g carbohydrate; 2 g protein; 0 g fiber; 89 mg sodium; 28 mg potassium.

Tzatziki Cucumber Dip

Combine ¾ cup nonfat **Greek-style yogurt** (*see Note, page 199*), ⅔ cup peeled, seeded and grated **cucumber**, 1 teaspoon extra-virgin **olive oil**, ½ teaspoon each minced **garlic** and **salt**.

MAKES ABOUT 1½ CUPS.

PER TABLESPOON: 6 calories; 0 g fat (0 g sat, 0 g mono); 0 mg cholesterol; 0 g carbohydrate; 1 g protein; 0 g fiber; 51 mg sodium; 5 mg potassium.

SOUPS ON THE SIDE

A simple pureed vegetable soup makes a great starter or accompaniment to a hearty salad for dinner. Plus leftovers are such a nice thing to have for lunch the next day. Here we give you the basic method and variations for carrot, potato, broccoli and pea soup.

Pureed Vegetable Soup

H✹W H⬆F H♥H

ACTIVE TIME: 35 to 45 minutes | **TOTAL:** 35 to 50 minutes
TO MAKE AHEAD: Cover and refrigerate for up to 4 days or freeze for up to 3 months.

- 1 tablespoon butter
- 1 tablespoon extra-virgin olive oil
- 1 medium onion, chopped
- 1 stalk celery, chopped
- 2 cloves garlic, chopped
- 1 teaspoon chopped fresh thyme *or* parsley
     Vegetable of choice (*see variations, right*)
     Water (*see variations, right, for amounts*)
- 4 cups reduced-sodium chicken broth, "no-chicken" broth (*see Note, page 198*) *or* vegetable broth
- ½ cup half-and-half (optional)
- ½ teaspoon salt
     Freshly ground pepper to taste

1. Heat butter and oil in a Dutch oven over medium heat until the butter melts. Add onion and celery; cook, stirring occasionally, until softened, 4 to 6 minutes. Add garlic and thyme (or parsley); cook, stirring, until fragrant, about 10 seconds.

2. Stir in vegetable of choice. Add water and broth; bring to a lively simmer over high heat. Reduce heat to maintain a lively simmer and cook until very tender. (*See variations, right, for timing.*)

3. Puree the soup in batches in a blender until smooth. (Use caution when pureeing hot liquids.) Stir in half-and-half (if using), salt and pepper.

MAKES 8 SERVINGS, ABOUT 1 CUP EACH.

Carrot Soup:

5 cups chopped carrots
2 cups water

Simmer for about 25 minutes.

PER SERVING: 77 calories; 3 g fat (1 g sat, 2 g mono); 4 mg cholesterol; 10 g carbohydrate; 3 g protein; 3 g fiber; 484 mg sodium; 396 mg potassium. **NUTRITION BONUS:** Vitamin A (269% daily value).

Potato Soup:

5 cups chopped peeled potatoes
2 cups water

Simmer for about 15 minutes.

PER SERVING: 128 calories; 3 g fat (1 g sat, 2 g mono); 4 mg cholesterol; 22 g carbohydrate; 4 g protein; 2 g fiber; 434 mg sodium; 460 mg potassium. **NUTRITION BONUS:** Vitamin C (15% daily value).

Broccoli Soup:

8 cups chopped broccoli (stems and florets)
2 cups water

Simmer for about 8 minutes.

PER SERVING: 69 calories; 4 g fat (1 g sat, 2 g mono); 4 mg cholesterol; 7 g carbohydrate; 4 g protein; 3 g fiber; 458 mg sodium; 348 mg potassium. **NUTRITION BONUS:** Vitamin C (80% daily value), Vitamin A (23% dv), Folate (21% dv).

Pea Soup:

6 cups peas (fresh *or* frozen)
½ cup water

Simmer for 1 minute.

PER SERVING: 131 calories; 3 g fat (1 g sat, 2 g mono); 4 mg cholesterol; 18 g carbohydrate; 7 g protein; 6 g fiber; 431 mg sodium; 419 mg potassium. **NUTRITION BONUS:** Vitamin C (28% daily value), Folate & Vitamin A (18% dv).

Carrot Soup

Pea Soup

Broccoli Soup

Potato Soup

BUILD A BETTER SIDE SALAD

Add a salad to your meal to pack more vegetable servings into your day. Make salads with a variety of colors to get an array of healthful nutrients. These mix-and-match salad ideas will re-invigorate your salad routine. **Pick from each category to build a delicious salad that serves 4.**

Start with 4 cups of greens:

Arugula is an aromatic green that lends a peppery mustard flavor to salads. Find it in bags or bunches near other salad greens in the supermarket.

Belgian endive has compact, slender, elongated heads with cream-colored leaves that have yellow or pink tips.

Butterhead lettuces (Boston and **Bibb)** are soft, buttery-textured lettuces with mild flavor. Lettuce heads are medium-large and the leaves are very tender.

Escarole is a type of chicory that has tender, broad, pale green leaves that can be eaten raw in salads or lightly cooked in soups, pasta or as a side dish.

Leaf lettuces are lettuces that grow leaves from a single stalk rather than forming a tight head. Find red or green varieties at most supermarkets.

Radicchio heads have thick purple-red leaves streaked with white veins. Radicchio's firm texture stands up well to dressing. Try it along with other salad greens to add color and to balance its bitter flavor.

Romaine is the lettuce of choice for Caesar salad. It grows in tall, cylindrical heads of narrow, crisp leaves.

Spinach is a tender, mild-flavored green. Baby spinach is immature or young spinach—it's harvested earlier than large-leaved mature spinach. Be sure to remove the tough stems from mature spinach before using.

Add a total of 1 cup of vegetables:

Artichoke hearts (canned), chopped
Beets, raw, shredded, or cooked *or* canned pickled, diced
Bell pepper, diced
Broccoli *or* cauliflower, chopped
Cabbage (red), shredded
Carrots, shredded
Corn kernels, fresh *or* thawed frozen
Cucumbers, sliced
Onion (red), slivered
Peas, thawed frozen
Radishes, sliced
Scallions, sliced
Snow peas, thinly sliced
Tomatoes, diced, *or* grape *or* cherry tomatoes, halved

Sprinkle up to ½ cup of add-ons on top:

Avocado, diced
Bacon, cooked, crumbled
Beans (canned), rinsed
Cheese, such as blue, feta, Cheddar, Parmesan, Asiago *or* Swiss, shredded *or* crumbled
Croutons, whole-wheat (*see Note, page 198*)
Eggs, hard-cooked (*see Note, page 199*), chopped
Dried fruit, such as raisins, currants *or* cranberries, *or* chopped dried apricots, pineapple *or* mangoes
Nuts, toasted (*see Note, page 199*), chopped
Olives, chopped *or* sliced
Orange *or* grapefruit segments

Toss with ¼ cup dressing (*opposite*):

Basic Vinaigrette
Blue Cheese Dressing
Buttermilk Ranch Dressing
Caesar Dressing
Ginger-Orange Dressing

DRESSING RECIPES

Cover and refrigerate any dressing for up to 3 days.

Basic Vinaigrette:

Whisk ⅔ cup extra-virgin **olive oil**, ½ cup **red-wine vinegar**, 1½ teaspoons finely chopped **garlic** and 1½ teaspoons **Dijon mustard**, and **salt** & **pepper** to taste in a small bowl. *Makes about 1 cup, 84 calories per tablespoon.*

Blue Cheese Dressing:

Whisk ¼ cup crumbled **blue cheese** and 2 tablespoons each reduced-fat **sour cream** and low-fat **mayonnaise** in a small bowl. Stir in ¼ cup nonfat *or* low-fat **buttermilk** and 1 tablespoon each **white-wine vinegar**, chopped fresh **parsley** and **scallions**. Season to taste with **salt** and **pepper**. *Makes ¾ cup, 18 calories per tablespoon.*

Buttermilk Ranch Dressing:

Whisk ½ cup nonfat *or* low-fat **buttermilk**, ¼ cup low-fat **mayonnaise**, 2 tablespoons **white-wine vinegar**, ½ teaspoon **granulated garlic**, and **salt** & **pepper** to taste in a small bowl until smooth. Stir in ⅓ cup chopped fresh **herbs**, such as chives, tarragon, basil *or* dill. *Makes about 1 cup, 8 calories per tablespoon.*

Caesar Dressing:

Mash 1 minced **garlic** clove and ¼ teaspoon **salt** in a medium bowl with the back of a spoon to form a paste. Add ¼ cup **lemon juice**, 2 tablespoons low-fat **mayonnaise**, 2 teaspoons **Dijon mustard**, 1½ teaspoons **anchovy paste** or to taste (optional) and **pepper** to taste; whisk to combine. Slowly drizzle in 3 tablespoons **oil**, whisking constantly. Add ¼ cup grated **Asiago cheese** and whisk to combine. *Makes 1 cup, 67 calories per tablespoon.*

Ginger-Orange Dressing:

Whisk 1½ teaspoons freshly grated **orange zest**, ¾ cup **orange juice**, ¼ cup **canola oil**, 3 tablespoons minced **scallions**, 1 tablespoon minced fresh **ginger**, ¾ teaspoon minced **garlic**, and **salt** & **pepper** to taste in a small bowl until well blended (or shake in a small jar). *Makes 1 cup, 21 calories per tablespoon.*

5 SALADS TO TRY

1. Leaf lettuce + chopped broccoli + diced tomatoes + dried cranberries + Basic Vinaigrette

2. Arugula + shredded carrots + diced bell pepper + whole-wheat croutons + Blue Cheese Dressing

3. Spinach + diced avocado + chopped cauliflower + slivered red onion + Buttermilk Ranch Dressing

4. Romaine + sliced radishes + sliced cucumbers + chopped hard-boiled eggs + Caesar Dressing

5. Butter lettuce + thinly sliced snow peas + orange segments + chopped toasted almonds + Ginger-Orange Dressing

VEGETABLE-ROASTING GUIDE

Roasting vegetables is a quick, easy way to give them tons of rich flavor with barely any work. Here's how:
To roast vegetables: Preheat oven to 450°F. Prepare the vegetable of your choice (*see instructions below*). Toss with 4 teaspoons extra-virgin olive oil (or canola oil), ½ teaspoon salt and ¼ teaspoon pepper—or with any of the seasoning combinations (*opposite*). Follow roasting times below.

VEGETABLE	AMOUNT FOR 4 SERVINGS	ROASTING TIME	ANALYSIS PER SERVING
Beets & Turnips	1 ½ pounds, greens removed, ends trimmed, peeled, cut into 1-inch pieces or wedges	20-25 minutes	*beets:* 116 calories; 16 g carbohydrate; 5 g fiber *turnips:* 90 calories; 11 g carbohydrate; 3 g fiber
Broccoli & Cauliflower	1 pound, cut into 1-inch florets	15-20 minutes	*broccoli:* 74 calories; 6 g carbohydrate; 3 g fiber *cauliflower:* 71 calories; 6 g carbohydrate; 3 g fiber
Brussels Sprouts	1 pound, outer leaves removed, stem trimmed; larger ones quartered, smaller ones halved	15-20 minutes	91 calories; 10 g carbohydrate; 4 g fiber
Butternut Squash	2 pounds, peeled, seeded, cut into 1-inch pieces	25-35 minutes	120 calories; 20 g carbohydrate; 6 g fiber
Cabbage, Savoy	1 ½ pounds (1 small head), cored, cut into 1-inch squares	15-20 minutes	83 calories; 9 g carbohydrate; 5 g fiber
Carrots & Parsnips	1 ½ pounds, peeled or scrubbed, woody core removed from parsnips; cut into ¼-inch slices	20-25 minutes	*carrots:* 105 calories; 15 g carbohydrate; 4 g fiber *parsnips:* 138 calories; 23 g carbohydrate; 5 g fiber
Fennel	2 large bulbs, stalks and fronds trimmed from the bulb, the bulb cored and cut into 1-inch wedges	25-30 minutes	79 calories; 9 g carbohydrate; 4 g fiber
Green Beans	1 pound, stem ends trimmed	15-20 minutes	78 calories; 8 g carbohydrate; 4 g fiber
Sweet Potatoes	1 ½ pounds, scrubbed (peeled if desired), cut into 1-inch pieces or wedges	20-25 minutes	196 calories; 35 g carbohydrate; 6 g fiber

10 WAYS TO SEASON ROASTED VEGETABLES

Toss prepared vegetables (*see chart, opposite*) with any of these easy flavor combinations.

1 Cardamom-Butter:

Before roasting: Toss the vegetables with 3 teaspoons melted **butter**, 1 teaspoon **canola oil**, ¾ teaspoon ground **cardamom** and ½ teaspoon **salt**.

2 Chile-Garlic & Soy:

Before roasting: Toss the vegetables with 4 teaspoons extra-virgin **olive oil** (*or* canola oil), 1 tablespoon each **chile-garlic sauce** (*see Note, page 198*) and reduced-sodium **soy sauce** and ⅛ teaspoon ground **white pepper**.

3 Chili-Lime:

Before roasting: Toss the vegetables with 4 teaspoons **canola oil**, ¾ teaspoon each **chili powder** and ground **cumin** and ½ teaspoon **salt**. *After roasting:* Toss with 2 tablespoons chopped fresh **cilantro** and **lime juice** to taste.

4 Garlic-Thyme:

Before roasting: Toss the vegetables with 2 tablespoons extra-virgin **olive oil**, 1 tablespoon chopped fresh **thyme** (*or* 1 teaspoon dried), ¼ teaspoon each **salt** and freshly ground **pepper**. About 5 minutes before the vegetables are done, stir in ¼ cup thinly sliced **garlic** and continue roasting. *After roasting:* Toss with 2 tablespoons chopped **fennel fronds** if desired.

5 Ginger-Sesame:

Before roasting: Toss the vegetables with 2 tablespoons each **toasted sesame oil** and reduced-sodium **soy sauce**, 1 tablespoon each grated fresh **ginger** and minced **garlic**, 4 teaspoons **rice vinegar** and ½ teaspoon freshly ground **pepper**. *After roasting:* Toss with 1 tablespoon toasted **sesame seeds** (*see Note, page 199*).

6 Lemon-Herb:

Before roasting: Toss the vegetables with 4 teaspoons extra-virgin **olive oil** (*or* canola oil), 2 tablespoons chopped fresh **herbs**, such as marjoram, oregano, tarragon *and/or* rosemary (*or* 2 teaspoons dried), 1 teaspoon freshly grated **lemon zest**, ½ teaspoon **salt** and ¼ teaspoon freshly ground **pepper**. *After roasting:* Toss with 1 tablespoon **lemon juice** if desired.

7 Maple:

Before roasting: Toss the vegetables with 2 tablespoons pure **maple syrup**, 1 tablespoon melted **butter**, 1½ teaspoons **lemon juice**, ½ teaspoon **salt** and freshly ground **pepper** to taste.

8 Mediterranean:

Before roasting: Toss the vegetables with 4 teaspoons extra-virgin **olive oil**, 2 minced **garlic** cloves and ¼ teaspoon **salt**. *After roasting:* Toss with ½ teaspoon freshly grated **lemon zest**, 1 tablespoon **lemon juice**, 10 pitted sliced **black olives**, 1 teaspoon dried **oregano** and 2 teaspoons rinsed **capers** (optional).

9 Moroccan:

Before roasting: Toss the vegetables with 2 tablespoons extra-virgin **olive oil**, 2 minced **garlic** cloves, 1 teaspoon each **paprika** (preferably sweet Hungarian) and ground **cumin** and ½ teaspoon **salt**.

10 Spicy Orange:

Before roasting: Toss the vegetables with 4 teaspoons extra-virgin **olive oil**, the **zest of 1 orange**, ½ teaspoon **salt** and ¼-½ teaspoon **crushed red pepper**.

VEGETABLE-STEAMING GUIDE

Steamed vegetables can't be beat for simplicity or health. Serve them plain with a drizzle of olive oil and a little salt and pepper or season them with one of our flavor combinations (*opposite*).

To steam vegetables: Bring an inch of water to a steady boil in a large saucepan over high heat. Prepare the vegetable of your choice and place in a steamer basket in the saucepan. Cover and steam until just tender. See the chart below for prep instructions and timing.

VEGETABLE	AMOUNT FOR 4 SERVINGS	STEAMING TIME	ANALYSIS PER SERVING
Asparagus	1½ pounds (1-2 bunches), trimmed	4 minutes	37 calories; 7 g carbohydrate; 3 g fiber
Beets	1½ pounds, greens removed, ends trimmed, peeled, cut into 1-inch pieces or wedges	10-15 minutes	75 calories; 17 g carbohydrate; 3 g fiber
Broccoli & Cauliflower	1 pound broccoli, 1½-2 pounds cauliflower (about 1 head), cut into 1-inch florets	5-6 minutes	*broccoli:* 32 calories; 6 g carbohydrate; 3 g fiber *cauliflower:* 39 calories; 7 g carbohydrate; 4 g fiber
Brussels Sprouts	1 pound, stems trimmed	6-8 minutes	41 calories; 8 g carbohydrate; 3 g fiber
Carrots	1½ pounds, cut into ⅛-inch-thick rounds	4 minutes	60 calories; 14 g carbohydrate; 5 g fiber
Green Beans	1 pound, trimmed	5 minutes	40 calories; 9 g carbohydrate; 4 g fiber
Potatoes (baby), red or Yukon Gold	1½ pounds, scrubbed	10-15 minutes	140 calories; 30 g carbohydrate; 2 g fiber
Snap Peas	1 pound, trimmed	4-5 minutes	53 calories; 9 g carbohydrate; 3 g fiber
Summer Squash	1½ pounds, cut into ¼-inch-thick rounds	4-5 minutes	27 calories; 6 g carbohydrate; 2 g fiber

10 WAYS TO PERK UP STEAMED VEGETABLES

Toss or top steamed vegetables (*see chart, opposite*) with any of these easy flavor combinations.

1 Bacon-Horseradish:

Combine 4 strips crisp-cooked **bacon**, finely chopped, ¼ cup reduced-fat **sour cream**, 2 teaspoons prepared **horseradish**, ¼ teaspoon **salt** and ⅛ teaspoon freshly ground **pepper**.

2 Caper & Parsley:

Combine ⅓ cup chopped **shallot**, ¼ cup flatleaf **parsley** leaves, 3 tablespoons rinsed **capers**, 2 tablespoons **white-wine vinegar**, 2 teaspoons extra-virgin **olive oil**, ¼ teaspoon each **salt** and freshly ground **pepper**.

3 Creamy Garlic:

Whisk ½ cup nonfat plain **yogurt**, 1 tablespoon extra-virgin **olive oil**, 1 tablespoon chopped fresh **parsley** (optional), ½ teaspoon each **garlic powder** and **kosher salt**, and freshly ground **pepper** to taste.

4 Fresh Tomato & Shallot:

Combine 2 chopped **tomatoes**, 1 minced **shallot**, 1 tablespoon each extra-virgin **olive oil** and **balsamic vinegar**, and **salt** & freshly ground **pepper** to taste.

5 Lemon-Dill:

Whisk 4 teaspoons chopped fresh **dill**, 1 tablespoon each minced **shallot**, extra-virgin **olive oil** and **lemon juice**, 1 teaspoon **whole-grain mustard**, ¼ teaspoon each **salt** and freshly ground **pepper**.

6 Mustard-Scallion:

Combine ¼ cup sliced **scallions**, 2 tablespoons **Dijon mustard**, 1 tablespoon **lemon juice**, and **salt** & freshly ground **pepper** to taste.

7 Orange-Almond:

Whisk 1 teaspoon extra-virgin **olive oil**, ½ teaspoon freshly grated **orange zest**, ¼ teaspoon **salt** and freshly ground **pepper** to taste; toss with steamed vegetables and top with ¼ cup toasted **sliced almonds** (*see Tip, page 199*).

8 Sesame-Orange:

Combine 3 tablespoons **orange juice**, 2 teaspoons **sesame oil**, ¼ teaspoon each **salt** and freshly ground **pepper**. Add 2 teaspoons toasted **sesame seeds** (*see Tip, page 199*).

9 Spicy Asian:

Combine 3 tablespoons each chopped **red bell pepper**, chopped **red onion** and **rice-wine vinegar** (*or* distilled white vinegar), 1 tablespoon **sesame oil**, 2 teaspoons **light brown sugar**, 1 teaspoon **crushed red pepper** and **salt** to taste.

10 Tarragon Cream:

Whisk 2 tablespoons each low-fat **mayonnaise** and low-fat plain **yogurt** (*or* nonfat or low-fat buttermilk), 1 tablespoon chopped fresh **tarragon** (*or* 1 teaspoon dried), ¼ teaspoon **salt**, and freshly ground **pepper** to taste.

POTATO-COOKING GUIDE

We love potatoes because they're satisfying, versatile, cheap and delicious. They're also nutritious—potatoes are rich in vitamin C and potassium and offer some fiber, especially when eaten with the skin on, so you can include them in a healthy diet. Here are some easy ways to enjoy potatoes—roasted, mashed or baked.

ROASTED POTATOES

Preheat oven to 450°F. Cut 2 pounds scrubbed **potatoes** (peeled if desired) into ¾-inch chunks. Toss in a large roasting pan with 1 tablespoon extra-virgin **olive oil**, ½ teaspoon **salt** and ¼ teaspoon **pepper**. Roast potatoes in upper third of oven, stirring occasionally, until golden brown and tender, 30 to 35 minutes. Makes 6 servings, 134 calories.

Toss prepared potatoes with one of these seasoning blends *before* roasting:

1 Cumin:

1 teaspoon ground cumin, ½ teaspoon ground coriander and a pinch of cayenne pepper

2 Lemon-Oregano:

1 teaspoon each freshly grated lemon zest and dried oregano

3 Mustard-Rosemary:

1 tablespoon each Dijon mustard and chopped fresh rosemary

Or toss potatoes *after* they're roasted with one of these:

1 Herbs:

2 tablespoons chopped fresh herbs, such as parsley *or* dill

2 Salt & Vinegar:

A sprinkling of malt vinegar (*or* white vinegar) and coarse salt

MASHED POTATOES

Scrub and peel 2 pounds all-purpose **potatoes** and cut into chunks. Place the potatoes in a large heavy saucepan. Add water to cover and season with **salt**. Bring to a boil. Reduce heat to medium, cover, and cook until the potatoes are very tender, 10 to 15 minutes. When the potatoes are done, drain in a colander and return to the pan. Place the pan over low heat and shake for about 1 minute to dry the potatoes. Mash the potatoes. *Makes 6 servings, 119 calories.*

Try these ideas for flavored mashed potatoes:

1 Cheddar-Chive:

Stir into mashed potatoes: 1 cup shredded extra-sharp Cheddar cheese, 2/3 cup buttermilk (*or* low-fat plain yogurt), 3 tablespoons sliced fresh chives (*or* scallion greens), salt & pepper to taste.

2 Garlic Mashed:

Cook 6 peeled garlic cloves with the potatoes. *After mashing:* Add 2/3 cup buttermilk (*or* low-fat plain yogurt), 2 teaspoons melted butter, salt & pepper to taste.

3 Goat Cheese:

Stir into mashed potatoes: 2/3 cup buttermilk (*or* low-fat plain yogurt), 2 teaspoons melted butter, 3 ounces crumbled goat cheese, salt & pepper to taste.

4 Herbed:

Stir into mashed potatoes: 2/3 cup buttermilk (*or* low-fat plain yogurt), 2 teaspoons extra-virgin olive oil, 3 tablespoons minced fresh chives *and/or* thyme, salt & pepper to taste.

5 Parsley-Buttermilk:

Stir into mashed potatoes: 1/3 cup buttermilk (*or* low-fat plain yogurt), 2 minced scallions, 1/4 cup minced parsley, 2 tablespoons butter, salt & pepper to taste.

BAKED POTATOES

Scrub 1 medium russet **potato** per person and pierce in several places with a fork. Place the potatoes in the microwave and cook on Medium, turning once or twice, until soft, about 20 minutes. (Or use the "potato setting" on your microwave and cook according to the manufacturer's directions.) Alternatively, bake potatoes directly on the center rack in a 400°F oven until tender, 45 to 60 minutes. *Per potato, 219 calories.*

Top each baked potato with one of the following:

1 Curry-Spiced:

1 tablespoon nonfat plain yogurt mixed with 2 teaspoons chopped scallions, 1/4 to 1/2 teaspoon curry powder and 1/4 teaspoon salt.

2 Feta & Olive:

1 tablespoon crumbled feta cheese, 2 teaspoons chopped fresh herbs and 1 teaspoon chopped black olives.

3 Salsa:

1 tablespoon each prepared salsa and Monterey Jack cheese and 1 teaspoon reduced-fat sour cream.

4 Scallion-Ranch:

1 tablespoon low-fat ranch dressing and 2 teaspoons chopped scallions.

5 Tomato-Pesto:

1 tablespoon prepared pesto and 1 chopped small plum tomato.

GRAIN-COOKING GUIDE

Start with **1 cup uncooked grain**; serving size is ½ cup cooked. See the chart below for prep instructions and timing.

GRAIN	LIQUID (WATER/BROTH)	DIRECTIONS	YIELD	ANALYSIS PER ½-CUP SERVING
BARLEY (Pearl)	2½ cups	Bring barley and liquid to a boil. Reduce heat to low and simmer, covered, 35-50 minutes.	3-3½ cups	97 calories; 22 g carbohydrate; 3 g fiber
BULGUR (see Note, page 199)	1½ cups	Bring bulgur and liquid to a boil. Reduce heat to low; simmer, covered, until tender and most of the liquid has been absorbed, 10-15 minutes.	2½-3 cups	76 calories; 17 g carbohydrate; 4 g fiber
COUSCOUS (Whole-wheat)	1¾ cups	Bring liquid to a boil; stir in couscous. Remove from heat and let stand, covered, for 5 minutes. Fluff with a fork.	3-3½ cups	70 calories; 15 g carbohydrate; 2 g fiber
POLENTA (Cornmeal)	4⅓ cups	Bring cold water and 1 teaspoon salt to a boil. Slowly whisk in cornmeal until smooth. Reduce heat to low, cover and cook, stirring occasionally, until very thick and creamy, 10 to 15 minutes.	4-4⅓ cups	55 calories; 12 g carbohydrate; 1 g fiber
QUINOA (see Note, page 199)	2 cups	Rinse in several changes of cold water. Bring quinoa and liquid to a boil. Reduce heat to low and simmer, covered, until tender and most of the liquid has been absorbed, 15-20 minutes. Fluff with a fork.	3 cups	111 calories; 20 g carbohydrate; 3 g fiber
RICE Brown	2½ cups	Bring rice and liquid to a boil. Reduce heat to low and simmer, covered, until tender and most of the liquid has been absorbed, 40-50 minutes. Let stand for 5 minutes, then fluff with a fork.	3 cups	109 calories; 23 g carbohydrate; 2 g fiber
Wild	At least 4 cups	Cook rice in a large saucepan of lightly salted boiling water until tender, 45-55 minutes. Drain.	2-2½ cups	83 calories; 18 g carbohydrate; 1 g fiber

IN A HURRY? Make instant brown rice, quick-cooking barley or quick-cooking wild rice, ready in under 10 minutes (follow package directions).

10 WAYS TO JAZZ UP WHOLE GRAINS

Add any of these flavor combinations to grains after they're cooked (*see chart, opposite*).

1 Apricot Nut:

Stir into cooked grains: ⅓ cup chopped **dried apricots**, ¼ cup chopped toasted **nuts**, such as walnuts, pecans *or* pistachios, 3 tablespoons **orange juice**, 1 teaspoon extra-virgin **olive oil**, and **salt** & freshly ground **pepper** to taste.

2 Lime-Cilantro:

Stir into cooked grains: ⅔ cup coarsely chopped fresh **cilantro**, ⅓ cup chopped **scallions**, 2 tablespoons **lime juice**, and **salt** & freshly ground **pepper** to taste.

3 Mediterranean:

Stir into cooked grains: 1 chopped medium **tomato**, ¼ cup chopped **kalamata olives**, ½ teaspoon **herbes de Provence**, and **salt** & freshly ground **pepper** to taste.

4 Mint & Feta:

Stir into cooked grains: ¾ cup sliced **scallions**, ¼ cup each finely crumbled **feta cheese** and sliced fresh **mint**, and **salt** & freshly ground **pepper** to taste.

5 Parmesan & Balsamic:

Stir into cooked grains: ¼ cup freshly grated **Parmesan cheese**, 1 teaspoon **butter,** 2 teaspoons **balsamic vinegar**, and **salt** & freshly ground **pepper** to taste.

6 Parmesan-Dill:

Stir into cooked grains: ⅓ cup freshly grated **Parmesan cheese**, 2 tablespoons chopped fresh **dill**, 1 teaspoon freshly grated **lemon zest**, and **salt** & freshly ground **pepper** to taste.

7 Peas & Lemon:

Stir into cooked grains: 1 cup frozen **peas**; cover and let stand for 5 minutes. Stir in 3 tablespoons chopped fresh **parsley**, 1½ teaspoons extra-virgin **olive oil**, 1 teaspoon freshly grated **lemon zest**, and **salt** & freshly ground **pepper** to taste.

8 Spicy & Sweet Sesame-Soy:

Stir into cooked grains: 3 tablespoons **rice-wine vinegar**, 1 tablespoon reduced-sodium **soy sauce**, 2 teaspoons each **sesame oil** and finely chopped fresh **ginger**, 1 teaspoon each **chile-garlic sauce** and **honey**, and ¼ cup chopped toasted **cashews**.

9 Spinach:

Stir into cooked grains: 3 cups sliced **baby spinach** (*or* arugula); cover and let stand for 5 minutes. Season with **salt** & freshly ground **pepper** to taste.

10 Tomato-Tarragon:

Stir into cooked grains: ¾ cup chopped **tomatoes**, 3 tablespoons minced fresh **tarragon** (*or* parsley *or* thyme), and **salt** & freshly ground **pepper** to taste.

Bulgur

Quinoa

Barley

8 DESSERTS & TREATS

Skip store-bought desserts and make healthier, inexpensive sweets at home. And dessert doesn't have to mean hours of baking. Just check out these Mocha Ice Pops—all you need is coffee and a couple other pantry ingredients to whip them up.

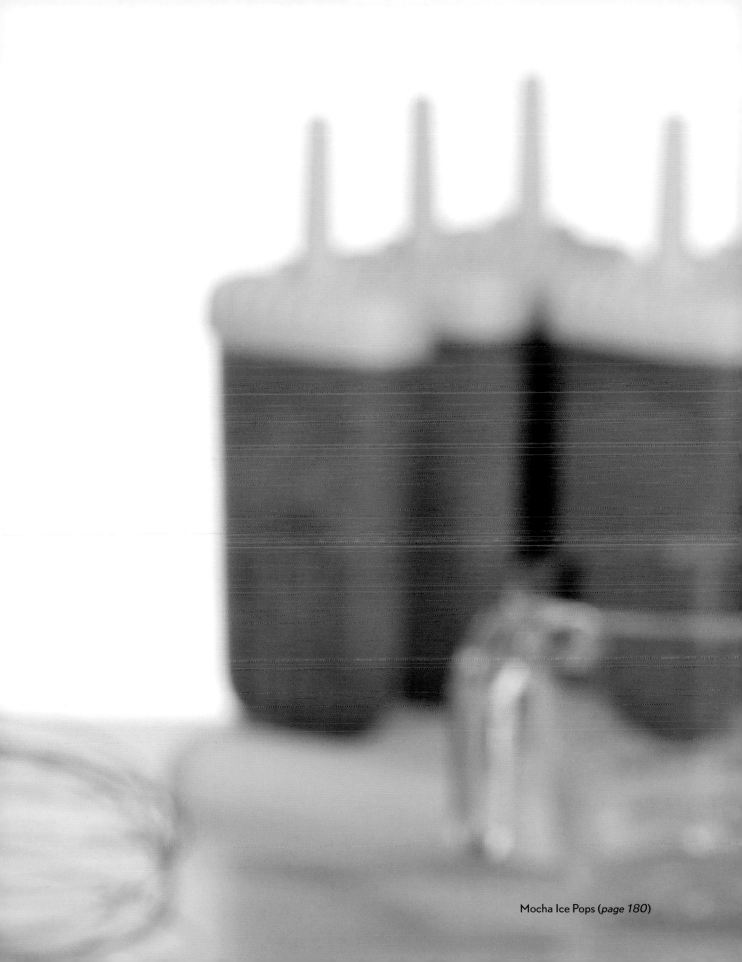

Mocha Ice Pops (*page 180*)

Enjoy these
Double Peanut
Butter Chocol
Chev

Double Peanut Butter-Chocolate Chewies

These soft chocolate cookies have a big peanut flavor since they use peanut butter and peanut butter chips. Package them up to give to a friend or send one in a lunchbox for dessert.

ACTIVE TIME: 1 hour

TOTAL: 1 1/2 hours

TO MAKE AHEAD: Store in an air-tight container for up to 3 days or freeze for up to 3 months.

PER COOKIE:

115 calories; 6 g fat (1 g sat, 1 g mono); 12 mg cholesterol; 13 g carbohydrate; 3 g protein; 1 g fiber; 102 mg sodium; 33 mg potassium.

NOTE:

Turbinado sugar is steam-cleaned raw cane sugar. It's coarse-grained and light brown in color, with a slight molasses flavor. Find it in the natural-foods section of large supermarkets or at natural-foods stores.

1	cup chunky natural peanut butter
1/4	cup canola oil
1/2	cup packed dark brown sugar
1/2	cup granulated sugar
2	large eggs
3	tablespoons low-fat plain yogurt
1	tablespoon vanilla extract
3/4	cup all-purpose flour
1/3	cup unsweetened cocoa powder
1/4	cup rolled oats
1	teaspoon baking soda
1/2	teaspoon salt
1/4	cup semisweet chocolate chips
1/4	cup trans-fat-free peanut butter chips, such as Sunspire
1/4	cup turbinado sugar (*see Note*)

1. Preheat oven to 350°F.

2. Beat peanut butter, oil, brown sugar and granulated sugar in a large bowl with an electric mixer on medium speed until the sugars are blended. Beat in eggs, yogurt and vanilla until combined.

3. Whisk flour, cocoa, oats, baking soda and salt in a medium bowl. With the mixer on low speed, gradually add the dry ingredients to the peanut butter mixture until blended. (It will be sticky.) Stir in chocolate and peanut butter chips.

4. Using a small cookie scoop or slightly rounded tablespoons of dough, place cookies 2 inches apart on ungreased cookie sheets.

5. Dip the bottom of a glass in water and then in turbinado sugar. Use the sugared glass to flatten the cookies slightly, leaving a thin layer of sugar on top, rewetting the glass as needed.

6. Bake the cookies in batches until they are just set and the tops appear cracked, 8 to 10 minutes. (Do not overbake or they will be dry.) Cool on the baking sheet for 2 minutes before transferring to a wire rack to cool.

MAKES 3 DOZEN COOKIES.

ACTIVE TIME: 40 minutes

TOTAL: 3 ½ hours (including cooling time)

TO MAKE AHEAD: Prepare the crust (Step 1), wrap tightly and refrigerate for up to 2 days or freeze for up to 6 months.

EQUIPMENT: Parchment paper

PER SERVING:

253 calories; 10 g fat (3 g sat, 4 g mono); 28 mg cholesterol; 37 g carbohydrate; 3 g protein; 2 g fiber; 163 mg sodium; 49 mg potassium.

NOTE:

Whole-wheat pastry flour is milled from soft wheat. It has less gluten-forming potential than regular whole-wheat flour and helps ensure a tender result in delicate baked goods while providing the nutritional benefits of whole grains. Available in large supermarkets and in natural-foods stores. Store in the freezer.

·········· **SAVE** ··········

Purchase whole-wheat pastry flour in the bulk section of natural-foods stores so you can get just what you need. If you have leftover flour, store it in the refrigerator or freezer.

Mom's Apple Squares

This apple square has a flaky, buttery crust and a sweet apple filling. It was inspired by a less-healthy version made with trans-fat-laden shortening in the crust. We replaced it with a mixture of canola oil and butter and swapped out half the all-purpose flour for whole-wheat pastry flour for a little fiber. They are best enjoyed slightly warm. Gently reheat any leftovers in the oven or toaster oven to recrisp the crust.

1 ¼	cups whole-wheat pastry flour (*see Note*)
1 ¼	cups all-purpose flour
2	tablespoons sugar, plus ¾ cup, divided
¾	teaspoon salt
¼	teaspoon baking powder
4	tablespoons cold unsalted butter
5	tablespoons canola oil
⅓	cup ice water
1	large egg, separated
4	cups thinly sliced firm tart apples, such as Granny Smith, Empire *or* Cortland, peeled if desired
1	teaspoon ground cinnamon

1. Whisk whole-wheat flour, all-purpose flour, 2 tablespoons sugar, salt and baking powder in a large bowl. Cut butter into small pieces and quickly rub them into the dry ingredients with your fingers until smaller but still visible. Add oil and toss with a fork to combine. Whisk water and egg yolk in a small bowl. Add to the flour mixture and stir until it begins to come together. Knead the dough with your hands in the bowl a few times until it forms a ball. Divide the dough in half and shape into 5-inch disks. Wrap each in plastic and refrigerate for at least 1 hour.

2. Preheat oven to 400°F. Coat a 9-by-13-inch baking pan with cooking spray and line the bottom and sides with parchment paper.

3. Combine apples, the remaining ¾ cup sugar and cinnamon in a large bowl.

4. Roll one portion of dough between sheets of parchment or wax paper into a 9-by-13-inch rectangle. Peel off the top sheet and invert the dough into the prepared pan. Peel off the remaining paper. Trim the dough so it covers just the bottom of the pan. Spread the apple filling evenly over the dough. Using the parchment or wax paper, roll out the remaining dough, invert it over the filling and trim the edges so it just covers the filling. Whisk the egg white in a bowl until frothy and evenly brush over the top crust. Lightly sprinkle the crust with additional sugar, if desired.

5. Bake until golden brown and bubbling, 40 to 45 minutes. Let cool for at least 1 hour before cutting into 12 squares.

MAKES 12 SERVINGS.

ACTIVE TIME: 35 minutes

TOTAL: 2 hours

PER SERVING:

333 calories; 6 g fat (2 g sat, 2 g mono); 57 mg cholesterol; 60 g carbohydrate; 9 g protein; 1 g fiber; 236 mg sodium; 414 mg potassium.

NUTRITION BONUS:

Calcium (24% daily value).

H ♥ H

Bread Pudding with Bourbon Sauce

This classic Cajun dessert is a great way to turn stale bread into a luscious treat.

BREAD PUDDING

- 4 cups cubed day-old French bread (5 ounces)
- ¼ cup pecan halves
- 2 large eggs
- ¾ cup plus 2 tablespoons packed dark brown sugar
- 2 cups evaporated fat-free milk
- 1 tablespoon vanilla extract
- 1½ teaspoons ground cinnamon
- 1 teaspoon freshly grated nutmeg
- ½ cup raisins
- 3 teaspoons granulated sugar, divided
- 1 tablespoon butter

BOURBON SAUCE

- ⅓ cup evaporated fat-free milk
- ¼ cup granulated sugar
- 3 tablespoons bourbon
- 2 tablespoons nonfat plain yogurt

1. **To make bread pudding:** Preheat oven to 325°F. Spread bread cubes on a baking sheet and bake, stirring twice, until lightly toasted, about 10 minutes. Meanwhile, spread pecans in a pie plate and bake until fragrant, 8 to 10 minutes. Let cool and chop coarsely.

2. Whisk eggs and brown sugar in a large bowl. Blend in evaporated milk, vanilla, cinnamon and nutmeg. Stir in the toasted bread, pecans and raisins. Cover and refrigerate for at least 30 minutes or up to 1 hour.

3. Meanwhile, lightly coat a shallow 2-quart baking dish with cooking spray. Sprinkle with 1½ teaspoons granulated sugar. Melt butter in a small saucepan over low heat. Skim off froth and cook until it begins to turn light nutty brown, 1½ to 2 minutes. (Be careful not to burn the butter.) Transfer to a small bowl and let cool.

4. Pour the bread mixture into the prepared baking dish. Drizzle the browned butter over the top and sprinkle with the remaining 1½ teaspoons granulated sugar. Bake the pudding until firm in the center, 40 minutes. Increase the oven temperature to 425° and bake until the top is brown and puffed, 10 to 15 minutes more.

5. **To make bourbon sauce:** Meanwhile, place a deep mixing bowl, beaters and evaporated milk in the freezer to chill for 20 minutes. Beat the milk in the chilled bowl with an electric mixer until it is the consistency of whipped cream, 1 to 2 minutes. Gradually add ¼ cup granulated sugar, bourbon and yogurt and beat until thickened, several minutes more. Serve the sauce with the warm bread pudding.

MAKES 8 SERVINGS.

Old-Fashioned Gingerbread

Applesauce and buttermilk help keep this yummy spice cake moist even though it only contains ¼ cup oil. Serve plain, with a spoonful of raspberry jam or even a dollop of nonfat Greek-style yogurt.

ACTIVE TIME: 20 minutes

TOTAL: 1 hour

PER SERVING:

262 calories; 5 g fat (1 g sat, 3 g mono); 18 mg cholesterol; 50 g carbohydrate; 4 g protein; 2 g fiber; 335 mg sodium; 435 mg potassium.

NUTRITION BONUS:

Magnesium (17% daily value).

H ♥ H

NOTE:

Whole-wheat pastry flour is milled from soft wheat. It has less gluten-forming potential than regular whole-wheat flour and helps ensure a tender result in delicate baked goods while providing the nutritional benefits of whole grains. Available in large supermarkets and in natural-foods stores. Store in the freezer.

1½	cups whole-wheat pastry flour (*see Note*)
1	cup all-purpose flour
2	teaspoons baking soda
2	teaspoons ground ginger
1½	teaspoons ground cinnamon
½	teaspoon salt
1	large egg
½	cup packed dark brown sugar
¼	cup canola oil
1	cup molasses
½	cup applesauce
½	cup nonfat *or* low-fat buttermilk (*see Save tip*)

1. Preheat oven to 350°F. Coat an 8-by-12-inch baking pan with cooking spray.

2. Whisk whole-wheat flour, all-purpose flour, baking soda, ginger, cinnamon and salt in a bowl.

3. Beat egg, brown sugar and oil in a large bowl with an electric mixer on high speed until thick and creamy. Reduce speed to low and beat in molasses and applesauce.

4. Gently mix the dry ingredients and buttermilk into the egg mixture with a rubber spatula, making 3 additions of dry ingredients and 2 additions of buttermilk. (Do not overmix.)

5. Scrape the batter into the prepared pan. Bake until a skewer inserted in the center comes out clean, 35 to 45 minutes. Let cool slightly in the pan on a wire rack. Serve warm.

MAKES 12 SERVINGS.

···SAVE····················

If you won't be able to use a whole carton of buttermilk, don't worry: you have options. Leftover buttermilk can be stored in the freezer. Or you can get powdered buttermilk instead, which keeps in your refrigerator for months. Or skip buying buttermilk and substitute 1 cup milk mixed with 1 tablespoon lemon juice.

ACTIVE TIME: 20 minutes

TOTAL: 2 hours 20 minutes (including freezing time)

TO MAKE AHEAD: Cover and freeze the pie for up to 3 days.

EQUIPMENT: 9-inch deep-dish pie pan

PER SERVING:

231 calories; 5 g fat (1 g sat, 2 g mono); 4 mg cholesterol; 42 g carbohydrate; 4 g protein; 2 g fiber; 179 mg sodium; 149 mg potassium.

NUTRITION BONUS:

Vitamin A (81% daily value).

H✕W   H♥H

NOTE:

To soften **ice cream** quickly, microwave on Medium-Low for 30 to 60 seconds.

........**SAVE**........

Stock up on canned pumpkin during the holiday season when stores usually offer it at sale prices. It's loaded with antioxidants and dietary fiber and can be used throughout the year to make delicious, healthy soups, pasta sauces or even pumpkin ice cream.

Frozen Pumpkin Mousse Pie

While pumpkin pie deserves respect as a Thanksgiving icon, it's fun to shake up tradition. Surprise your family and friends with a frozen pie this year—it just might become one of their holiday favorites. And once you try this pie you may decide it's too good to just have at the holidays.

CRUST

30	small gingersnap cookies (about 7½ ounces)
2	tablespoons raisins
1	tablespoon canola oil

FILLING

1	cup canned pumpkin puree
⅓	cup packed brown sugar
½	teaspoon ground cinnamon
¼	teaspoon ground ginger
¼	teaspoon freshly grated nutmeg
2	pints (4 cups) low-fat vanilla ice cream, softened (*see Note*)

1. Preheat oven to 350°F. Coat a 9-inch deep-dish pie pan with cooking spray.

2. **To prepare crust:** Combine gingersnaps and raisins in a food processor and pulse until finely chopped. Add oil and pulse until blended. Press evenly into the bottom and up the sides of the prepared pan.

3. Bake the crust until set, about 10 minutes. Transfer to a wire rack to cool completely.

4. **To prepare filling:** Combine pumpkin, brown sugar, cinnamon, ginger and nutmeg in a large bowl and mix well. Add ice cream and stir until blended. Spoon the mixture into the cooled pie crust. Freeze until firm, at least 2 hours. Let the pie soften slightly in the refrigerator for 20 to 30 minutes before serving.

MAKES 10 SERVINGS.

Mango Pudding

Very ripe mangoes make this simple Chinese pudding sublime. Traditionally, agar-agar—a derivative of seaweed—is used as the thickener. We use more commonly available gelatin and add sweetened condensed milk for a touch of creaminess. Use a very fine sieve for the smoothest texture. The recipe can be cut in half to make 4 puddings instead of 8.

- 2   envelopes unflavored gelatin (4 1/2 teaspoons)
- 1/2   cup water
- 4-6   ripe mangoes, peeled and diced (*see Note, page 199*), *or* 5 cups diced frozen mango, thawed
- 1   14-ounce can nonfat sweetened condensed milk
- 4   tablespoons lime juice

1. Sprinkle gelatin over water in a small bowl; let stand until softened, about 1 minute. Microwave on High, uncovered, until the gelatin has completely dissolved but the liquid is not boiling, 10 to 20 seconds. (*Alternatively, bring 1/2 inch water to a gentle simmer in a small skillet. Set the bowl with the gelatin mixture in the simmering water until the gelatin has dissolved completely.*) Stir the mixture until smooth.

2. Place mango in a blender or food processor. Process until smooth. Push through a very fine sieve into a large measuring cup until you have 2 cups puree. (Reserve any extra fruit or puree for a smoothie or yogurt topping.) Whisk the mango puree, sweetened condensed milk and lime juice in a medium bowl. Slowly whisk in the softened gelatin mixture until well combined.

3. Lightly coat eight 6- to 10-ounce ramekins with cooking spray. Divide the pudding among the ramekins. Refrigerate until set, about 2 hours.

4. To serve, run a knife around the inside of each ramekin to loosen the pudding. Dip the bottom of the ramekin in hot water for 30 to 40 seconds, then invert onto a serving plate, holding ramekin and plate tightly together.

MAKES 8 SERVINGS.

ACTIVE TIME: 40 minutes

TOTAL: 2 hours 40 minutes (including 2 hours chilling time)

TO MAKE AHEAD: Refrigerate for up to 2 days.

EQUIPMENT: Eight 6- to 10-ounce ramekins

PER SERVING:

214 calories; 0 g fat (0 g sat, 0 g mono); 6 mg cholesterol; 49 g carbohydrate; 6 g protein; 2 g fiber; 56 mg sodium; 641 mg potassium.

NUTRITION BONUS:

Vitamin C (50% daily value), Potassium & Vitamin A (18% dv).

Mocha Ice Pops

H✱W H♥H

Whisk 2½ cups hot brewed **coffee**, 4 to 5 tablespoons **sugar** and 2 tablespoons unsweetened **cocoa powder** in a medium bowl until the sugar has dissolved. Whisk in 1 cup **half-and-half**, ¼ teaspoon **vanilla extract** and a pinch of **salt** until combined. Divide the mixture among freezer-pop molds. Insert the sticks and freeze until completely firm, about 6 hours. (*They will keep in the freezer for up to 3 weeks.*) Dip the molds briefly in hot water before unmolding. (*Photograph: page 168.*)

MAKES ABOUT 10 (3-OUNCE) FREEZER POPS.

PER SERVING: 54 calories; 3 g fat (2 g sat, 1 g mono); 9 mg cholesterol; 7 g carbohydrate; 1 g protein; 0 g fiber; 26 mg sodium; 77 mg potassium.

Grilled Dark Chocolate Sandwich

H✱W

Heat ¼ cup fat-free **evaporated milk** just until boiling. Add 3 ounces finely chopped bittersweet **chocolate**, let stand for 1 minute, then whisk until smooth. Let cool slightly. Spread 1½ tablespoons softened **butter** on one side each of 8 slices thin whole-wheat (*or* white) **sandwich bread**. Divide the chocolate mixture on the unbuttered side of 4 slices, leaving a little border. Press 3 tablespoons

bittersweet (*or* semisweet) **chocolate chips** (and 2 tablespoons chopped toasted **hazelnuts**, if desired) into the chocolate. Top with the remaining slices of bread, buttered-side up, and press lightly. Cook the sandwiches in a large nonstick skillet over medium-high heat for 1 to 2 minutes. Turn over, press with a spatula, and cook until nicely browned and the chocolate is barely melted, 30 seconds to 1 minute. Cut sandwiches in half and serve warm.

MAKES 8 SERVINGS, ½ SANDWICH EACH.

PER SERVING: 171 calories; 10 g fat (5 g sat, 0 g mono); 6 mg cholesterol; 20 g carbohydrate; 5 g protein; 3 g fiber; 142 mg sodium; 97 mg potassium.

Chocolate Crunch

H✱W H⬆F

Combine 1 cup **Wheat Chex cereal**, 1 cup **pretzel sticks** (broken in half), ¼ cup salted roasted **almonds** in a bowl. Melt 3 tablespoons bittersweet **chocolate chips**, drizzle over the Chex mixture; stir to combine. Spread the mixture on a wax paper-lined baking sheet and refrigerate until the chocolate is set. (*Refrigerate in an airtight container for up to 5 days.*)

MAKES 4 SERVINGS, ABOUT ¾ CUP EACH.

PER SERVING: 222 calories; 10 g fat (3 g sat, 3 g mono); 0 mg cholesterol; 32 g carbohydrate; 5 g protein; 4 g fiber; 394 mg sodium; 139 mg potassium. NUTRITION BONUS: Folate (53% daily value), Iron (33% dv).

Grilled Dark Chocolate Sandwich   **Chocolate Crunch**   **Rich Chocolate Sauce**

Toasted Oat & Apple Crumble

H↑F H♥H

Preheat oven to 350°F. Spread 1 cup **oats** on a baking sheet; bake, stirring occasionally, until lightly browned, 15 to 18 minutes. Cool. Combine with ½ cup each **whole-wheat flour** and **all-purpose flour**, 1 cup **light brown sugar**, 1½ teaspoons ground **cinnamon**, ¼ teaspoon **salt**, ¼ cup thawed frozen **apple juice concentrate** and 2 tablespoons **canola oil** in a large bowl. Spread 6 cups peeled and thickly sliced **apples** in a lightly oiled 2-quart baking dish. Sprinkle the oat mixture on top. Bake for 35 to 40 minutes.

MAKES 8 SERVINGS.

PER SERVING: 268 calories; 5 g fat (0 g sat, 3 g mono); 0 mg cholesterol; 57 g carbohydrate; 3 g protein; 3 g fiber; 75 mg sodium; 190 mg potassium.

Quick Cherry Sauce

Bring two 10-ounce bags frozen pitted **cherries** (preferably sour) and ⅔ cup each **sugar** and **water** to a boil in a medium saucepan over medium-high heat, stirring often. Stir ¼ cup **water** and 2 tablespoons **cornstarch** in a small bowl until smooth and stir into the boiling cherry mixture. Return to a boil, stirring constantly; cook until thickened, about 1 minute. Remove from heat and stir in ¼ cup **lemon juice**. (*Refrigerate for up to 1 week.*) Serve over ice cream, cake or Greek yogurt.

MAKES ABOUT 4 CUPS, FOR 24 SERVINGS.

PER SERVING: 36 calories; 0 g fat (0 g sat, 0 g mono); 0 mg cholesterol; 9 g carbohydrate; 0 g protein; 0 g fiber; 1 mg sodium; 33 mg potassium.

Rich Chocolate Sauce

Bring 1 cup low-fat **milk**, ½ cup each **sugar** and unsweetened **cocoa powder** and 1 tablespoon **butter** to a simmer in a small saucepan over medium heat, whisking constantly. Remove from heat; stir in 1½ ounces chopped bittersweet (*or* semisweet) **chocolate** and ½ teaspoon **vanilla extract** until it melts. Serve warm or let stand 10 minutes for a thicker sauce. (*Refrigerate for up to 1 week. Reheat in a saucepan over low heat, stirring often.*)

MAKES ABOUT 1⅔ CUPS.

PER TABLESPOON: 34 calories; 1 g fat (1 g sat, 0 g mono); 2 mg cholesterol; 6 g carbohydrate; 1 g protein; 1 g fiber; 5 mg sodium; 25 mg potassium.

Nut Praline Topping

Preheat oven to 350°F. Line a baking sheet with foil and coat with cooking spray. Stir 1 cup coarsely chopped **pecans** (*or* walnuts) with 2 tablespoons packed **light brown sugar** and 1 tablespoon mild **honey** (*or* light corn syrup) in a small bowl until well coated. Spread out on the prepared baking sheet. Bake on the center rack, stirring occasionally, until the nuts are fragrant and lightly brown, 7 to 10 minutes. Let cool on a wire rack for 15 minutes. Crumble the praline into small pieces. (*Refrigerate for up to 1 month.*) Serve on ice cream or stirred into yogurt.

MAKES ABOUT 1¼ CUPS.

PER TABLESPOON: 46 calories; 4 g fat (0 g sat, 2 g mono); 0 mg cholesterol; 3 g carbohydrate; 1 g protein; 1 g fiber; 0 mg sodium; 25 mg potassium.

Caramelized Bananas

H↑F

Halve 2 medium-small firm **bananas** lengthwise. Melt ½ tablespoon **butter** in a nonstick skillet over medium-high heat. Add 3 tablespoons **light brown sugar** and lay the banana slices on top, cut side up. Cook undisturbed for 20 seconds, then add ¼ cup **dark rum** (*or* orange juice) and ⅛ teaspoon ground **cinnamon**. Cook for 10 seconds, then turn carefully and cook for 45 to 60 seconds more, basting with the pan sauce. Serve with a ½-cup scoop of low-fat **vanilla ice cream** (*or* frozen yogurt) each.

MAKES 2 SERVINGS.

PER SERVING: 372 calories; 7 g fat (4 g sat, 1 g mono); 28 mg cholesterol; 61 g carbohydrate; 5 g protein; 3 g fiber; 58 mg sodium; 521 mg potassium. **NUTRITION BONUS:** Potassium & Vitamin C (15% daily value).

9 BUDGET BASICS

Looking for more ways to save? Try packing lunch and snacks to take with you to school or work. Learn how to make some basics at home, such as chicken broth, jam, pizza dough and beans. And find our handy list of essential healthy ingredients you should keep stocked in your pantry.

Couscous & Fruit Salad (*page 186*)

QUICK BREAKFASTS

Maple-Nut Granola

H❈W   H♥H

Preheat oven to 275°F. Combine 5 cups old-fashioned rolled **oats**, 1 cup unsweetened **coconut chips** (*or* flakes), ½ cup each sliced **almonds**, chopped **pecans** and **light brown sugar**, ⅓ cup each unsalted **pumpkin seeds** and unsalted **sunflower seeds** in a large bowl. Combine ½ cup each pure **maple syrup** and **water** and ¼ cup **canola oil** and pour over the oat mixture; stir until well combined. Spread the mixture into a large (12-by-15-inch) roasting pan or large rimmed baking sheet. Bake for 1½ hours, stirring halfway through, until golden brown and beginning to crisp. Remove from oven; stir in ½ cup each **dried cranberries** and **raisins**. Let cool completely before storing. (*Store in an airtight container for up to 2 weeks.*)

MAKES 10 CUPS.

PER ½-CUP SERVING: 251 calories; 12 g fat (3 g sat, 4 g mono); 0 mg cholesterol; 32 g carbohydrate; 6 g protein; 4 g fiber; 3 mg sodium; 111 mg potassium.

Maple-Nut Granola

Banana-Walnut Oatmeal

H❈W   H↑F   H♥H

Heat 1 cup low-fat **milk**, ¾ cup water and a pinch of **salt** in a medium saucepan until almost boiling. Add 1 cup **quick-cooking oats** and cook, stirring, until creamy, 1 to 2 minutes. Remove from the heat and stir in 1 mashed very ripe **banana** and 1 tablespoon **maple syrup**. Sprinkle with 1 tablespoon chopped **walnuts**.

MAKES 2 SERVINGS, ABOUT 1 CUP EACH.

PER SERVING: 308 calories; 7 g fat (2 g sat, 2 g mono); 8 mg cholesterol; 54 g carbohydrate; 11 g protein; 6 g fiber; 142 mg sodium. **NUTRITION BONUS:** Magnesium (33% daily value), Calcium (17% dv).

Egg & Salmon Sandwich

H❈W   H♥H

Heat ½ teaspoon extra-virgin **olive oil** in a small nonstick skillet over medium heat. Add 1 tablespoon finely chopped **red onion** and cook, stirring, until it begins to soften, about 1 minute. Add 2 large beaten **egg whites**, pinch of **salt** and ½ teaspoon rinsed and chopped **capers** (if desired), and cook, stirring constantly, until whites are set, about 30 seconds. To make the sandwich, split and toast 1 **whole-wheat English muffin** and top it with the egg whites, 1 ounce **smoked salmon** and 1 slice **tomato**.

MAKES 1 SANDWICH.

PER SERVING: 213 calories; 5 g fat (1 g sat, 2 g mono); 7 mg cholesterol; 25 g carbohydrate; 19 g protein; 3 g fiber; 669 mg sodium; 219 mg potassium. **NUTRITION BONUS:** Source of omega-3s.

Egg & Salmon Sandwich

Breakfast Parfait

H✚W   H♥H

Top ¾ cup low-fat **cottage cheese** (*or* low-fat plain yogurt) with 1 cup **pineapple chunks** (*or* papaya chunks *or* cling peaches). Sprinkle with 2 teaspoons **toasted wheat germ**.

MAKES 1 SERVING.

PER SERVING: 222 calories; 2 g fat (1 g sat, 1 g mono); 7 mg cholesterol; 29 g carbohydrate; 23 g protein; 3 g fiber; 24 mg sodium; 370 mg potassium. NUTRITION BONUS: Vitamin C (132% daily value), Folate (17% dv).

Cranberry Muesli

H✚W   H♥H

Combine ½ cup each low-fat plain **yogurt** and unsweetened (*or* fruit-juice-sweetened) **cranberry juice**, 6 tablespoons old-fashioned rolled **oats** (*not* quick-cooking or steel cut), 2 tablespoons **dried cranberries**, 1 tablespoon each unsalted **sunflower seeds** and **wheat germ**, 2 tea-spoons **honey**, ¼ teaspoon **vanilla extract** and ⅛ teaspoon **salt** in a medium bowl; cover and refrigerate for at least 8 hours and up to 1 day.

MAKES 2 SERVINGS, ABOUT ⅔ CUP EACH.

PER SERVING: 210 calories; 4 g fat (1 g sat, 1 g mono); 4 mg cholesterol; 37 g carbohydrate; 8 g protein; 3 g fiber; 190 mg sodium; 264 mg potassium.

Mixed Berry Smoothie

H✚W   H↑F   H♥H

Combine 1 cup **frozen mixed berries**, ½ **banana**, ½ cup **apple juice** and ¼ cup **silken tofu** in a blender; blend until smooth.

MAKES 1 SERVING.

PER SERVING: 276 calories; 3 g fat (0 g sat, 0 g mono); 0 mg cholesterol; 62 g carbohydrate; 6 g protein; 7 g fiber; 35 mg sodium; 589 mg potassium. NUTRITION BONUS: Vitamin C (45% daily value), Potassium (17% dv).

Breakfast Parfait   Cranberry Muesli   Mixed Berry Smoothie

PACK A LUNCH

Peanut Tofu Wrap

H✘W H↑F H♥H

Spread 1 tablespoon store-bought **Thai peanut sauce** on an 8-inch **whole-wheat flour tortilla.** Place 2 ounces thinly sliced **seasoned baked tofu,** ¼ cup sliced **red bell pepper** and 8 thinly sliced **snow peas** in the center; fold the sides over the filling and roll up.

MAKES 1 SERVING.

PER SERVING: 312 calories; 11 g fat (2 g sat, 0 g mono); 0 mg cholesterol; 33 g carbohydrate; 19 g protein; 5 g fiber; 863 mg sodium; 154 mg potassium. **NUTRITION BONUS:** Vitamin C (90% daily value), Vitamin A (50% dv), Iron (20% dv), Calcium (15% dv).

Rice & Lentil Salad

H✘W H↑F H♥H

Whisk 2 tablespoons each extra-virgin **olive oil,** sherry (*or* red-wine) **vinegar,** 1 tablespoon each finely chopped **shallot** and **Dijon mustard,** ½ teaspoon **paprika** (preferably smoked) and ¼ teaspoon each **salt** and **pepper** in a large bowl. Stir in 2 cups cooked **brown rice,** one 15-ounce can rinsed **lentils** (*or* 1⅓ cups cooked), 1 diced **carrot** and 2 tablespoons chopped fresh **parsley.**

MAKES 4 SERVINGS, ABOUT 1 CUP EACH.

PER SERVING: 250 calories; 8 g fat (1 g sat, 6 g mono); 0 mg cholesterol; 36 g carbohydrate; 8 g protein; 8 g fiber; 272 mg sodium; 151 mg potassium. **NUTRITION BONUS:** Vitamin A (60% daily value), Folate (42% dv).

BBQ Chicken Sandwich

H✘W H♥H

Combine ½ cup shredded cooked **chicken,** ¼ cup shredded **carrots** and 2 tablespoons **barbecue sauce** in a bowl. Spread 2 teaspoons **light ranch dressing** on a small **whole-wheat sandwich bun.** Top with the chicken mixture and a piece of **romaine lettuce.**

MAKES 1 SERVING.

PER SERVING: 328 calories; 8 g fat (1 g sat, 2 g mono); 62 mg cholesterol; 39 g carbohydrate; 26 g protein; 4 g fiber; 771 mg sodium; 464 mg potassium. **NUTRITION BONUS:** Vitamin A (100% daily value).

Couscous & Fruit Salad

H✘W H↑F H♥H

Whisk 2 tablespoons each **olive oil** and **orange juice,** 1 tablespoon **cider vinegar,** 2 teaspoons minced **shallot,** ¼ teaspoon **salt** and **pepper** to taste. Combine with 2 cups

Peanut Tofu Wrap

Rice & Lentil Salad

BBQ Chicken Sandwich

each cooked **whole-wheat couscous** and **ripe summer fruit** and 2 tablespoons toasted sliced **almonds**.

MAKES 4 SERVINGS, ABOUT ¾ CUP EACH.

PER SERVING: 256 calories; 9 g fat (1 g sat, 6 g mono); 0 mg cholesterol; 40 g carbohydrate; 7 g protein; 7 g fiber; 146 mg sodium; 140 mg potassium. **NUTRITION BONUS:** Fiber (28% daily value), Vitamin C (20% dv).

Couscous & Fruit Salad

Shrimp Cobb Salad

H✖W H♥H

Combine 3 cups chopped **hearts of romaine**, 5 **grape** (*or* cherry) **tomatoes**, ¼ cup sliced **cucumber**, 1 sliced **hard-boiled egg** and 5 cooked peeled **shrimp** (31-40 per pound) in a bowl. Season with **black pepper**. Serve tossed with 2 tablespoons **light blue cheese dressing**.

MAKES 1 SERVING.

PER SERVING: 256 calories; 13 g fat (3 g sat, 2 g mono); 343 mg cholesterol; 12 g carbohydrate; 24 g protein; 4 g fiber; 513 mg sodium; 776 mg potassium. **NUTRITION BONUS:** Vitamin A (270% daily value), Vitamin C (78% dv), Folate (59% dv), Iron & Potassium (22% dv), Magnesium (15% dv).

Shrimp Cobb Salad

Curried Chicken Pitas

H✖W H⬆F H♥H

Combine 6 tablespoons nonfat plain **yogurt**, ¼ cup low-fat **mayonnaise** and 1 tablespoon **curry powder** in a large bowl. Toss with 2 cups cubed cooked **chicken**, 1 diced firm **pear**, 1 diced **celery** stalk, ½ cup **dried cranberries** and ¼ cup toasted sliced **almonds**. Fill 4 small **whole-wheat pitas** with 1 cup **chicken salad** and ½ cup **sprouts** each.

MAKES 4 SERVINGS.

PER SERVING: 323 calories; 7 g fat (1 g sat, 3 g mono); 58 mg cholesterol; 41 g carbohydrate; 27 g protein; 6 g fiber; 352 mg sodium; 372 mg potassium. **NUTRITION BONUS:** Magnesium (17% daily value).

Curried Chicken Pitas

EASY SNACKS

Fruit Salad with Lime Yogurt

H✂W H♥H

Cut 1 large ripe **honeydew** melon into 1½-inch chunks; hull 1 pint **strawberries** and cut in half. Toss the melon and strawberries in a large bowl with ¼ cup **lime juice** and 2 tablespoons **sugar**. Let stand for 15 minutes, stirring occasionally. Meanwhile combine 2 cups nonfat plain **yogurt**, ¼ cup **sugar**, 1 tablespoon each freshly grated **lime zest** and **lime juice** in a small bowl, stirring until the sugar is dissolved. Cover and refrigerate until chilled. (*The Lime Yogurt will keep in the refrigerator for up to 2 days.*) Serve the fruit salad with the Lime Yogurt.

MAKES 8 SERVINGS, ABOUT 1½ CUPS EACH.

PER SERVING: 135 calories; 0 g fat (0 g sat, 0 g mono); 1 mg cholesterol; 33 g carbohydrate; 4 g protein; 2 g fiber; 63 mg sodium; 441 mg potassium. NUTRITION BONUS: Vitamin C (100% daily value).

Zesty Bean Dip & Chips

H✂W H♥H

Combine ¼ cup fat-free canned **refried beans**, 1 tablespoon **salsa**, 1½ teaspoons chopped fresh **cilantro** and 1 minced **scallion** (optional) in a bowl. Serve with 1 ounce (about 10) **tortilla chips**.

MAKES 1 SERVING.

PER SERVING: 199 calories; 8 g fat (1 g sat, 2 g mono); 0 mg cholesterol; 30 g carbohydrate; 5 g protein; 4 g fiber; 452 mg sodium; 273 mg potassium.

Chile-Lime Tortilla Chips

Position racks in the middle and lower third of oven; preheat to 375°F. Coat twelve 6-inch **corn tortillas** on both sides with cooking spray; cut into quarters. Place in an even layer on 2 large baking sheets. Combine 2 tablespoons **lime juice** and ½ teaspoon **chili powder** in a small bowl. Brush the mixture on each tortilla wedge and sprinkle with **salt**. Bake the tortillas, switching the baking sheets halfway through, until golden and crisp, 15 to 20 minutes.

MAKES 6 SERVINGS, 8 CHIPS EACH.

PER SERVING: 142 calories; 2 g fat (0 g sat, 0 g mono); 0 mg cholesterol; 29 g carbohydrate; 2 g protein; 2 g fiber; 169 mg sodium; 10 mg potassium.

Cottage Cheese Veggie Dip

H✂W H♥H

Combine ½ cup low-fat **cottage cheese** and ¼ teaspoon **lemon pepper**. Serve with ½ cup each baby **carrots** and **snow** (*or* snap) **peas**.

MAKES 1 SERVING.

PER SERVING: 119 calories; 2 g fat (1 g sat, 0 g mono); 10 mg cholesterol; 14 g carbohydrate; 14 g protein; 2 g fiber; 531 mg sodium; 200 mg potassium. NUTRITION BONUS: Vitamin A (170% daily value), Vitamin C (30% dv), Calcium (26% dv).

Edamame-Ginger Dip

H✂W H♥H

Cook 8 ounces (1½ cups) frozen shelled **edamame** according to package directions. Puree in a food processor with ¼ cup **water**, 2 tablespoons reduced-sodium **soy sauce**, 1 tablespoon each minced fresh **ginger**, **rice vinegar** and **tahini**, 1 **garlic** clove, ⅛ teaspoon **salt** and **hot sauce** to taste. Chill for 1 hour. Serve with rice crackers.

MAKES 1½ CUPS, FOR 6 SERVINGS.

PER ¼ CUP & 6 RICE CRACKERS: 108 calories; 3 g fat (0 g sat, 1 g mono); 0 mg cholesterol; 14 g carbohydrate; 5 g protein; 2 g fiber; 214 mg sodium; 32 mg potassium.

EatingWell Pimiento Cheese

Combine 1½ cups shredded reduced-fat **Cheddar cheese**, ¼ cup low-fat **mayonnaise**, one 4-ounce jar sliced **pimientos** (drained and chopped), 2 tablespoons minced **scallions** and **hot sauce** to taste. Serve with whole-grain crackers.

MAKES 1½ CUPS, FOR 12 SERVINGS.

PER 2 TABLESPOONS & 2 CRACKERS: 87 calories; 5 g fat (2 g sat, 1 g mono); 9 mg cholesterol; 7 g carbohydrate; 4 g protein; 1 g fiber; 220 mg sodium; 30 mg potassium.

Mediterranean Picnic Snack

H✱W H♥H

Cut 1 slice of crusty **whole-wheat bread** into bite-size pieces. Combine with 10 **cherry tomatoes**, ¼ ounce sliced aged **cheese** and 6 oil-cured **olives** in a portable container.

MAKES 1 SERVING.

PER SERVING: 196 calories; 9 g fat (2 g sat, 1 g mono); 5 mg cholesterol; 22 g carbohydrate; 7 g protein; 4 g fiber; 679 mg sodium; 473 mg potassium. NUTRITION BONUS: Vitamin C (100% daily value).

Spiced Chickpea "Nuts"

Rinse one 15-ounce can **chickpeas**. Blot dry and toss with 1 tablespoon extra-virgin **olive oil**, 2 teaspoons ground **cumin**, 1 teaspoon dried **marjoram** and ¼ teaspoon each ground **allspice** and **salt.** Spread on a rimmed baking sheet. Bake at 450°F in the upper third of the oven, stirring once or twice, until browned and crunchy, 25 to 30 minutes. Let cool on the baking sheet for 15 minutes.

MAKES 1 CUP, FOR 4 SERVINGS.

PER SERVING: 103 calories; 5 g fat (0 g sat, 3 g mono); 0 mg cholesterol; 14 g carbohydrate; 4 g protein; 5 g fiber; 303 mg sodium; 2 mg potassium.

Edamame-Ginger Dip

EatingWell Pimiento Cheese

Mediterranean Picnic Snack

Spiced Chickpeas "Nuts"

MAKE IT AT HOME

Here are a few basics to make at home if you have the time. Making your own helps you save even more.

Chicken Broth

ACTIVE TIME: 15 minutes | **TOTAL:** 2¼ hours | **TO MAKE AHEAD:** Refrigerate for up to 2 days or freeze for up to 6 months.

Use the leftovers of a roasted chicken dinner (after removing the meat) to make savory broth.

  2 roast chicken carcasses, meat removed
  1 onion, quartered
  1 carrot, quartered
  1 stalk celery, quartered
  6 cloves garlic, unpeeled
  1 gallon water

     Several sprigs fresh parsley and thyme
  1 teaspoon black peppercorns
  1 teaspoon salt

Place carcasses in a large pot. Add onion, carrot, celery, garlic and water. Bring to a boil, skimming foam. Reduce heat to low and add herbs, peppercorns and salt; simmer gently, uncovered, for 2 hours. Strain through a fine sieve into a large bowl. (Discard solids.) Let cool slightly, then refrigerate until cold. Skim off fat.

MAKES ABOUT 3 QUARTS.

Vegetable Broth

ACTIVE TIME: 15 minutes | **TOTAL:** 45 minutes | **TO MAKE AHEAD:** Cover and refrigerate for up to 2 days or freeze for up to 6 months.

While there are some commercial vegetable broths we like, nothing beats the fresh flavor of homemade.

  4 quarts water
  4 carrots, chopped
  2 medium onions, chopped
  2 leeks, trimmed, washed and chopped
  2 stalks celery
  8 mushrooms, sliced
  1 tomato, quartered
  5 sprigs fresh parsley
  3 sprigs fresh thyme *or* ½ teaspoon dried
 ½ teaspoon kosher salt
  1 bay leaf

Place all ingredients in a large pot. Bring to a boil over medium heat and cook, uncovered, for 30 minutes, skimming foam. Strain through a fine sieve. (Discard solids.)

MAKES ABOUT 4 QUARTS.

ANALYSIS NOTE: After straining and skimming, broth has negligible calories and nutrients except sodium (120 mg per cup).

Easy Whole-Wheat Pizza Dough

ACTIVE TIME: 20 minutes | **TOTAL:** 1 hour 20 minutes | **TO MAKE AHEAD:** Prepare through Step 3, cover the bowl with plastic wrap and refrigerate for up to 1 day. Or tightly wrap the unrisen dough in oiled plastic wrap and freeze for up to 3 months. Defrost the dough in the refrigerator overnight. Let refrigerated (or previously frozen) dough stand at room temperature for 1 hour before using.

This homemade pizza dough requires only one rising, so it's quicker to make than you might expect.

- 3/4 cup plus 2 tablespoons lukewarm water (105-115°F)
- 1 package active dry yeast (2 1/4 teaspoons)
- 1 teaspoon sugar
- 1/2 teaspoon salt
- 1 cup whole-wheat flour
- 1 cup bread flour *or* all-purpose flour
- 2 tablespoons yellow cornmeal

1. Stir water, yeast, sugar and salt in a large bowl; let stand until the yeast has dissolved, about 5 minutes. Stir in whole-wheat flour, bread flour (or all-purpose flour) and cornmeal until the dough begins to come together.
2. Turn the dough out onto a lightly floured work surface. Knead until smooth and elastic, about 10 minutes. (*Alternatively, mix the dough in a food processor. Process until it forms a ball, then process for 1 minute to knead.*)
3. Place the dough in an oiled bowl and turn to coat. (*To make individual pizzas, see Variation, below.*) Cover with a clean kitchen towel and set aside in a warm, draft-free place until doubled in size, about 1 hour.
4. When you're ready to make your pizza, turn the dough out onto a lightly floured surface. Dust the top with flour; dimple with your fingertips to shape into a thick, flattened circle—don't worry if it's not perfectly symmetrical. Then use a rolling pin to roll into a circle about 14 inches in diameter.

MAKES 1 POUND PIZZA DOUGH.

PER POUND: 970 calories; 5 g fat (1 g sat, 1 g mono); 0 mg cholesterol; 200 g carbohydrate; 36 g protein; 22 g fiber; 1,152 mg sodium; 782 mg potassium.

INDIVIDUAL VARIATION: After kneading, divide the dough into 4 or 6 equal balls. Brush with oil and place 3 inches apart on a baking sheet. Cover and set aside until doubled in size, about 1 hour. Roll each portion into a 6-to-8-inch circle.

HOW TO COOK BEANS

By cooking your own dried beans, you save money, reduce sodium and get better flavor. Freeze any extra cooked beans to use in soups, salads and dips. The range of time for cooking beans varies widely with the age and type of beans selected.

Equivalents

A pound of dried beans (about 2 cups) will yield 5 to 6 cups cooked beans.

One 19-ounce can yields about 2 cups cooked beans; a 15-ounce can, about 1 1/2 cups.

Soaking

To soak or not to soak? Soaking beans before cooking helps them to cook more evenly and cuts down on the total cooking time. So if you've planned ahead, soak them. If you don't have time, skip the soaking, but plan to cook the beans longer. Fresher beans, which are less dry, need less soaking time than beans that were harvested more than a year ago.

OVERNIGHT SOAK: Rinse and pick over the beans, then place in a large bowl with enough cold water to cover them by 2 inches. Let the beans soak for at least 8 hours or overnight. Drain.

QUICK SOAK: Rinse and pick over the beans, then place them in a large pot with enough cold water to cover them by 2 inches. Bring to a boil. Boil for 2 minutes. Remove from the heat and let stand, covered, for 1 hour; drain.

Cooking

CONVENTIONAL METHOD: Place the drained, soaked beans in a large pot and add enough cold water to cover them by 2 inches (about 2 quarts of water for 1 pound of beans). Bring to a boil, skimming off any debris that rises to the surface. Reduce the heat to low and simmer gently, stirring occasionally, until the beans are tender, 20 minutes to 3 hours (cooking time will vary with the type and age of bean). Add salt to taste.

SLOW-COOKER METHOD: Place the drained, soaked beans in a slow cooker and pour in 5 cups boiling water. Cover and cook on high until tender, 2 to 3 1/2 hours. Add salt to taste, and cook 15 minutes more.

HOMEMADE JAM

Here's a basic recipe for making lower-sugar jam. Make it with your favorite fruit or whatever's ripe at the moment.

Fresh Fruit Jam

ACTIVE TIME: 20-40 minutes | **TOTAL:** 20-40 minutes (depending on the type of fruit) | **TO MAKE AHEAD:** Store in the refrigerator for up to 3 weeks or in the freezer for up to 1 year. | **EQUIPMENT:** Six to eight 8-ounce canning jars

12　cups prepared fresh fruit, peeled if desired (*see "The Fruit Basket"*)

1-2　cups granulated sugar *or* brown sugar (*see "Sugar Subs"*)

½　cup water

1　1.75-ounce packet "no sugar needed" pectin (*see "About Pectin"*)

1. Combine fruit, sugar to taste and water in a Dutch oven. Bring to a vigorous boil and crush fruit with a potato masher until desired consistency. Add pectin in a steady stream, stirring constantly. Stir until the pectin is dissolved. Bring to a full rolling boil (a boil that cannot be "stirred down"), stirring constantly. Boil, stirring, for 1 minute. Remove from the heat.

2. Ladle the jam into clean canning jars to within ½ inch of the rim. Wipe rims clean. Cover with lids. Let the jars stand at room temperature until set, about 24 hours, before refrigerating or freezing.

MAKES 6-8 CUPS.

PER TABLESPOON (STRAWBERRY): 12 calories; 0 g fat (0 g sat, 0 g mono); 0 mg cholesterol; 3 g carbohydrate; 0 g protein; 0 g fiber; 1 mg sodium; 32 mg potassium.

The Fruit Basket

How to Prep & Measure

Berries: Remove stems; hull strawberries. Measure whole. Cherries: Remove stems and pits; halve. Measure halves. Peaches, Nectarines & Plums: Peel if desired. Cut into ½-inch pieces; discard pits. Measure pieces. Apples, Pears & other fruit: Peel if desired. Quarter, remove seeds and cut into ½-inch pieces. Measure pieces.

Sugar Subs

In this recipe, ¾ cup maple syrup (*or* honey) *or* ½-1 cup Splenda Granular can be used in place of 1 cup sugar.

About Pectin

We tested Fresh Fruit Jam with "No sugar needed" pectin from Ball and Sure-Jell. We prefer this to regular pectin because you can adjust the amount of added sugar. Regular pectin cannot be used in its place because it requires more sugar to ensure a proper set. Although Sure-Jell's instructions indicate that you cannot use less sugar than called for in their recipes, we had successful results using less (as indicated in our recipes).

FREEZING FRESH PRODUCE

Freezing produce is one of the easiest ways to preserve the abundance.
Follow our easy guide to enjoy your harvest throughout the year.

Vegetable Prep

The best vegetables to freeze are fresh from the garden and at their peak ripeness. Start by trimming and washing your vegetables under cold water. Remove any stems and wash under cold water. Peel if necessary. Cut to desired size, if necessary, according to their intended use (for example, carrots can be left whole or dice them for an easy soup addition).

Blanch vegetables before freezing. It stops the enzymes that keep vegetables ripening, helps get rid of dirt and bacteria, brightens color, slows vitamin and mineral loss, and wilts and softens the vegetables so they are easier to pack.

TO BLANCH VEGETABLES: Bring a large pot of water to a boil (use at least 1 gallon of water per pound of vegetables). Add the vegetables to the water. Once the water returns to a boil, cook the vegetables 1 to 2 minutes. Remove the vegetables from the boiling water with a slotted spoon and transfer them immediately to a bowl of ice water until they are completely chilled. Drain the vegetables well.

Tomatoes do not need to be blanched before freezing. Just wash, peel (if desired) and remove the core.

Fruit Prep

Freeze fruit that is at its peak ripeness. Fruit like raspberries and cherries will be best just after harvesting, while peaches and plums might need to ripen before freezing. Also, only prepare enough fruit for a few containers at a time if the fruit is prone to browning.

Wash and dry the fruit thoroughly. Remove and discard any pieces that are green or rotting. Remove any pits or cores. Smaller fruits, such as berries, can be frozen whole. Cut larger fruits to desired size.

Choosing Containers

Frozen food can develop off flavors as a result of contact with air. Prevent this by choosing containers that are moisture- and vapor-proof. Opt for glass jars, freezer bags or other plastic containers that are designed for storing frozen foods. If using plastic bags, be sure to remove as much air as possible before sealing. A vacuum sealer is also useful for removing air and preserving quality.

Packing

There are two kinds of packing: solid-pack and loose-pack. To solid-pack fruit or vegetables, place the prepared produce in the desired container and freeze. Solid-packing conserves space and is useful when planning to use large batches of frozen vegetables or fruit at one time. To loose-pack, freeze one layer of fruit or vegetables on a baking sheet. Once the produce is frozen, transfer it to the storage container. Loose-packing takes up more space, but it is easier to remove just the amount desired, such as a handful of peas or a cup of raspberries.

Be sure to leave about 1 inch of head space (open space at the top of the freezer container) when solid-packing produce, as foods expand as they freeze. When loose-packing frozen foods, headspace is not necessary as the foods are already frozen. Moisture or food on the sealing edges of the container will prevent proper sealing, so wipe all edges clean before sealing. Label each container with the name and date packaged. Most frozen produce will keep for 8 to 12 months.

Freezing Fresh Herbs

Tender herbs, such as basil, chives, cilantro, dill, mint and parsley, are best suited to freezing. Blanching them first helps capture their fresh flavor. Drop into boiling water for several seconds, then with a slotted spoon or tongs, transfer to a bowl of ice water to chill for several seconds more. Blot dry with paper towels. Spread a single layer of the blanched herbs on a wax paper-lined baking sheet, cover loosely with plastic and freeze until solid, about 1 hour. Transfer to plastic freezer bags. Blanched herbs can be frozen for up to 4 months and can be chopped while still frozen before using in soups, stews and sauces.

GROWING GREENS IN A CONTAINER

Greens love cool weather, so take advantage of the spring and fall seasons to grow them. Here are some tips to get you started growing greens.

Garden Soil: Till or mix compost or aged bagged manure into your soil before sowing seeds. Compost adds nitrogen, which helps support leafy green plants.

Container Soil: If you are planting in a container, use organic potting soil that's enriched with compost.

Starting Seeds: Most greens will grow easily from seed; simply bury the seeds ½ inch in the soil, then tamp and smooth the soil over the seeds. Mark the area you planted with a stick or plant tag.

Look for Growth: Seeds should germinate in a week, and will be ready for the salad bowl in 25 to 45 days.

Get a Jump-Start: If you don't want to start from seed, purchase young plants at a garden nursery and transplant directly into your garden or container.

WHEN TO BUY ORGANIC

Whether organic or conventional, fruits and vegetables are an essential part of a healthy diet. Though it's typically more expensive, the benefit of organic produce is that it is not treated with chemical pesticides. Pesticides can be absorbed into fruits and vegetables, and leave trace residues. The Environmental Working Group (EWG), a nonprofit, nonpartisan organization, pored over the results of nearly 87,000 USDA and FDA tests for pesticides on 47 popular produce items and identified the types of fruits and vegetables that were most likely to have higher trace amounts. If buying all organic isn't a priority—or a financial reality for you—you might opt to buy organic specifically when you're selecting foods that are most heavily contaminated with pesticide and insecticide residues. Use these lists from the EWG to help you shop.

The Dirty Dozen: Most Commonly Contaminated

Apples, Bell peppers, Carrots, Celery, Cherries, Grapes (imported), Kale, Lettuce, Nectarines, Peaches, Pears, Strawberries

A Clean Dozen: Least Commonly Contaminated

Asparagus, Avocado, Cabbage, Eggplant, Kiwi, Mango, Onions, Papaya, Pineapple, Sweet corn (frozen), Sweet peas (frozen), Watermelon

Fertilize & Water: Fertilize young seedlings with seaweed-based organic fertilizer (found at garden centers). Keep the roots and the soil moist yet not oversaturated. Dry soil adds stress to the plants; soil that is too wet will weaken the plants.

Harvest Time: Many greens are "cut and come again." Just harvest the greens, leave the roots and keep watering, and they will sprout another set of greens. Harvest just above the soil line with scissors in order to keep the leaves clean and soil-free. Shake off any loose soil or grit.

GARDENING & SEED SOURCES
Buy seeds at your local garden center, supermarket or hardware store. If you're having trouble finding a specific variety check The Cook's Garden, *cooksgarden.com*, or Johnny's Selected Seeds, *johnnyseeds.com*. For gardening tools or containers like the one shown here, visit the Gardener's Supply website, *gardeners.com*.

THE HEALTHY PANTRY

While a good shopping list is the key to a quick and painless trip to the supermarket, a well-stocked pantry is the best way to ensure you'll have everything you need to cook once you get home. Our Healthy Pantry includes many of the items you need to prepare the recipes in this book plus a few other ingredients that will make impromptu meals easier.

Oils, Vinegars & Condiments

Oils: extra-virgin olive, canola

Vinegars: balsamic, red-wine, white-wine, rice, cider

Asian condiments: reduced-sodium soy sauce, fish sauce, hoisin sauce, oyster sauce, chile-garlic sauce, toasted sesame oil

Barbecue sauce

Hot sauce

Worcestershire sauce

Mustard: Dijon, whole-grain

Ketchup

Mayonnaise, low-fat

Flavorings

Salt: kosher, iodized table

Black peppercorns

Herbs and spices, assorted dried

Onions

Garlic, fresh

Ginger, fresh

Olives: Kalamata, green

Capers

Anchovies or anchovy paste

Lemons, limes, oranges

Dry Goods

Pasta, whole-wheat (assorted shapes)

Barley: pearl, quick-cooking

Bulgur

Couscous, whole-wheat

Quinoa

Rice: brown, instant brown, wild

Dried beans and lentils

Flour: whole-wheat, whole-wheat pastry (store opened packages in the refrigerator or freezer), all-purpose

Rolled oats

Cornmeal

Breadcrumbs: plain dry, coarse whole-wheat

Crackers, whole-grain

Unsweetened cocoa powder

Bittersweet chocolate

Sweeteners: granulated sugar, brown sugar, honey, pure maple syrup

Canned & Bottled Goods

Broth: reduced-sodium beef, chicken and/or vegetable (*or see page 190 for broth recipes*)

Clam juice

"Lite" coconut milk

Tomatoes, tomato paste

Beans: black, cannellini, kidney, pinto, great northern, chickpeas, lentils

Chunk light tuna

Wild Pacific salmon

Wine: red, white or nonalcoholic

Madeira

Sherry, dry

Nuts, Seeds & Fruits

(Store opened packages of in the refrigerator or freezer.)

Nuts: walnuts, pecans, almonds, hazelnuts, peanuts, pine nuts

Natural peanut butter

Seeds: pepitas, sesame seeds, sunflower seeds

Tahini (sesame paste)

Dried fruits: apricots, prunes, cherries, cranberries, dates, figs, raisins

Refrigerator Items

Milk, low-fat or nonfat

Buttermilk or buttermilk powder

Yogurt, plain and/or vanilla, low-fat or nonfat

Sour cream, reduced-fat or nonfat

Parmesan cheese, good-quality

Cheddar cheese, sharp

Eggs (large) or egg substitute, such as Egg Beaters

Orange juice

Tofu, water-packed

Tortillas: corn, whole-wheat

Freezer Basics

Fruit: berries, other fruit

Vegetables: peas, spinach, broccoli, corn

Ice cream or frozen yogurt, low-fat or nonfat

MENU PLAN & SHOPPING LIST

Not sure what to cook this week? Try this menu plan for a week's worth of delicious dinners from this book, plus a shopping list for all the ingredients you'll need.

SUNDAY	MONDAY	TUESDAY	WEDNESDAY	THURSDAY	FRIDAY	SATURDAY
Louisiana Catfish with Okra & Corn (p. 138), with mashed potatoes (p. 165)	Pork Chops au Poivre (p. 127), with roasted carrots (p. 160) brown rice and green salad	Cheese-&-Spinach-Stuffed Portobellos (p. 75), with whole-wheat fusilli	Sweet-&-Sour Chicken Drumsticks (p. 90), with roasted sweet potatoes (p. 160) and salad	Beef & Cabbage Stir-Fry with Peanut Sauce (p. 117), with brown rice	Salmon Rösti (p. 148), with steamed green beans (p. 162)	Black Bean Croquettes with Fresh Salsa (p. 79), and warm corn tortillas

Produce

- ❑ Avocado, 1 medium
- ❑ Cabbage, Savoy, 1 small head
- ❑ Carrots, 2 pounds
- ❑ Cilantro, 1 bunch
- ❑ Corn, 2 ears (or 2 cups frozen)
- ❑ Dill, 1 small bunch
- ❑ Garlic, 1 head
- ❑ Green beans, 1 pound
- ❑ Lemon, 1 medium
- ❑ Lettuce (whatever looks best), 2 heads
- ❑ Mint, 1 bunch
- ❑ Okra, 2 cups (or frozen)
- ❑ Onions, 1 medium yellow and 1 medium red
- ❑ Orange, 1 medium
- ❑ Portobello mushroom caps, 4 large
- ❑ Potatoes, 2 pounds
- ❑ Scallions, 1 bunch
- ❑ Shallot, 1 medium
- ❑ Spinach, 1 small bag
- ❑ Sweet potatoes, 1½ pounds
- ❑ Tomatoes, 4 medium

Dry Goods

- ❑ Black beans, two 15-ounce cans
- ❑ Breadcrumbs, plain dry, 1 small container
- ❑ Capers, 1 small jar
- ❑ Marinara sauce, 1 small jar
- ❑ Olives, kalamata
- ❑ Peanuts, roasted, 1 small jar
- ❑ Salmon, two 6- to 7-ounce cans
- ❑ Whole-grain mustard, 1 small jar
- ❑ Whole-wheat fusilli, 8 ounces

Spices

- ❑ Cajun (or Creole) seasoning
- ❑ Chili powder
- ❑ Coriander, ground
- ❑ Cumin, ground
- ❑ Italian seasoning

Meat & Seafood

- ❑ Beef sirloin, 1 pound
- ❑ Catfish fillets, 1 pound
- ❑ Chicken drumsticks, 8 (about 2 pounds)
- ❑ Pork chops, four 4-ounce boneless, ½ inch thick

Refrigerator

- ❑ Eggs
- ❑ Orange juice, 1 small container
- ❑ Parmesan cheese, 1 ounce
- ❑ Ricotta cheese, part-skim, 1 small container
- ❑ Sour cream, reduced-fat, 1 small container
- ❑ Tortillas, corn, 1 package

Freezer

- ❑ Corn, 1 small bag
- ❑ Hash-brown shredded potatoes, 12 ounces

Miscellaneous

- ❑ Brandy, ½ cup

Staples

- ❑ Black pepper
- ❑ Brown rice
- ❑ Canola oil
- ❑ Cider vinegar
- ❑ Cornstarch
- ❑ Flour, all-purpose
- ❑ Honey
- ❑ Olive oil
- ❑ Peanut butter, natural smooth
- ❑ Rice vinegar
- ❑ Salt
- ❑ Soy sauce, reduced-sodium
- ❑ Sugar

RECIPE GUIDELINES & NUTRIENT ANALYSES

How we test recipes

Each of our recipes is thoroughly tested in the EatingWell Test Kitchen. Our goal is to provide healthy, delicious recipes that are easy for anyone to cook at home.

- Recipes tested on average seven times each.
- Each recipe is tested by multiple testers.
- We test on both gas and electric stoves.
- We use a variety of tools and techniques.
- Testers shop major supermarkets to research availability of ingredients.
- Testers measure active and total time it takes to prepare each recipe.

How we price recipes

- Costs for ingredients come from *safeway.com* and *peapod.com*.
- Costs include every ingredient, even staples like salt, pepper and olive oil.
- Costs include only the amount of an ingredient used (for example, 1 teaspoon capers, not the entire jar).
- Garnishes and optional ingredients are not included in cost.
- Prices are our best estimate as of winter 2009.

How we analyze recipes

- All recipes are analyzed for nutrition content by a Registered Dietitian.
- We analyze for calories, total fat, saturated (sat) fat, monounsaturated (mono) fat, cholesterol, carbohydrate, protein, fiber, sodium and potassium, using The Food Processor SQL© Nutrition Analysis Software from ESHA Research, Salem, Oregon. (Note: Nutrition information is updated regularly. The current analyses appear with the recipes on *eatingwell.com*.)
- When a recipe provides 15 percent or more of the Daily Value (dv) of a nutrient, it is listed as a nutrition bonus. These values are FDA benchmarks for adults eating 2,000 calories a day.
- Recipes are tested and analyzed with iodized table salt unless otherwise indicated.

- We estimate that rinsing with water reduces the sodium in canned foods by 35%. (Readers on sodium-restricted diets can reduce or eliminate the salt in a recipe.)
- Garnishes and optional ingredients are not included in analyses.
- When a recipe gives a measurement range of an ingredient, we analyze the first amount.
- When alternative ingredients are listed, we analyze the first one suggested.
- We do not include trimmings or marinade that is not absorbed in analyses.

Recipe icons

Icons identify recipes that are most appropriate for certain eating goals. (For more on our nutritional analysis process and our complete guidelines on how we define each icon, visit *eatingwell.com/go/guidelines*.) A recipe marked…

H✖W [**Healthy Weight**] has reduced calories and limited saturated fat.

H⬆F [**High Fiber**] provides significant total fiber.

H♥H [**Healthy Heart**] has limited saturated fat.

⏱ is ready to eat in 45 minutes or less.

OTHER DEFINITIONS:

Active Time includes prep time (the time it takes to chop, dice, puree, mix, combine, etc. before cooking begins). It also includes the time spent tending something on the stovetop, in the oven or on the grill—and getting it to the table. If you can't walk away from it for more than 10 minutes, we consider it active time.

Total includes both active and inactive time and indicates the entire amount of time required for each recipe, start to finish.

To Make Ahead gives storage instructions for dishes that taste good made in advance. If special **Equipment** is needed to prepare a recipe, we tell you that too.

NOTES, TIPS & TECHNIQUES

Condiments & Flavorings

Anaheim chiles (a.k.a. New Mexico chiles) are 7 to 10 inches long, ripen from green to red and are mildly spicy. **Poblano peppers** (sometimes called pasilla peppers) are dark green in color, about 6 inches long and can be fiery or relatively mild; there's no way to tell until you taste them. The two can be used interchangeably and are found at most large supermarkets.

Chicken-flavored broth, a vegetarian broth despite its name, is preferable to vegetable broth in some recipes for its hearty, rich flavor. Sometimes called "no-chicken" broth, it can be found with the soups in the natural-foods section of most supermarkets.

Chile-garlic sauce (also labeled chili-garlic sauce, or paste) is a blend of ground chiles, garlic and vinegar. It can be found in the Asian section of large supermarkets and will keep for up to 1 year in the refrigerator.

Chinkiang is a dark, slightly sweet vinegar with a smoky flavor. It is available in many Asian specialty markets. If unavailable, balsamic vinegar is an acceptable substitute.

Fish sauce is a pungent condiment made from salted, fermented fish. Find it in the Asian section of large supermarkets and in Asian specialty markets. We use Thai Kitchen fish sauce, lower in sodium than other brands (1,190 mg per tablespoon), in our nutritional analyses.

Harissa is a fiery Tunisian chile paste commonly used in North African cooking. Find it at specialty-food stores, *mustaphas.com* or *amazon.com*. Harissa in a tube will be much hotter than that in a jar. You can substitute Chinese or Thai chile-garlic sauce for it. Try blending leftover harissa with mayonnaise for a spicy sandwich spread or stir it into hummus to give it a kick.

Paprika is a spice made from grinding dried red peppers. Paprika specifically labeled as "**Hungarian**" delivers a fuller, richer flavor than regular paprika. **Smoked paprika** is made from smoke-dried red peppers and adds earthy, smoky flavor. It can be used in many types of savory dishes. Look for different types of paprika in some large supermarkets, at *tienda.com* or *penzeys.com*.

Port is a fortified wine that provides depth of flavor in cooking. Look for it at a liquor store or in the wine section of the supermarket.

Red miso (akamiso) is a salty fermented paste made from barley or rice and soybeans. Find it in the refrigerated section near tofu. Use it for sauces, marinades or soup. Store miso in the refrigerator for up to 1 year.

Shao Hsing (or Shaoxing) is a seasoned rice wine available in the Asian or wine section of some supermarkets and in Asian food markets. Once opened, store in the refrigerator for up to 1 year.

Sherry is a type of fortified wine originally from southern Spain. Don't use the "cooking sherry" sold in many supermarkets—it can be surprisingly high in sodium. Instead, purchase dry or medium sherry that's sold with other fortified wines in your wine or liquor store.

Tahini is a thick paste of ground sesame seeds. Look for it in large supermarkets in the Middle Eastern section or near other nut butters. Store in the refrigerator for up to 6 months. If you have leftover tahini, try making your own hummus. Puree in a food processor: one 16-ounce can of chickpeas, 1/3 cup tahini, 3 to 4 tablespoons lemon juice and 2 to 3 tablespoons water, 1 minced garlic clove, and salt & pepper to taste.

Dry Goods

To make your own **breadcrumbs**, trim crusts from firm sandwich bread. Tear the bread into pieces and process in a food processor until coarse crumbs form. (To make fine dry breadcrumbs, process until very fine.) Spread on a baking sheet and bake at 250°F until dry, about 10 to 15 minutes. One slice of bread makes about 1/3 cup dry breadcrumbs. We like Ian's brand of coarse dry whole-wheat breadcrumbs, labeled "Panko breadcrumbs." Find them in the natural-foods section of large supermarkets.

To make homemade **croutons**: Toss 1 cup whole-grain bread cubes with 1 tablespoon extra-virgin olive oil, a pinch each of salt, pepper and garlic powder. Spread out on a baking sheet and toast at 350°F until crispy, turning occasionally, 15 to 20 minutes.

Soba (Japanese buckwheat noodles) and **rice noodles** can be found in the Asian section of most supermarkets.

Perfectly cooked rice can be tricky. To have the most success cooking **whole-grain rice**, we recommend using a pan with a tight-fitting lid, cooking on your coolest (or simmer) burner and making sure the rice is simmering at the "lowest bubble."

Whole-wheat pastry flour is milled from soft wheat. It has less gluten-forming potential than regular whole-wheat flour and helps ensure a tender result in delicate baked goods while providing the nutritional benefits of whole grains. Available in large supermarkets and in natural-foods stores. Store in the freezer.

Grains
See also Grain-Cooking Guide, page 166.

Bulgur is made by parboiling, drying and coarsely grinding or cracking wheat berries. Don't confuse bulgur with cracked wheat, which is simply that—cracked wheat. Since the parboiling step is skipped, cracked wheat must be cooked for up to an hour whereas bulgur simply needs a quick soak in hot water for most uses. Look for it in the natural-foods section of large supermarkets, near other grains, or online at *kalustyans.com, buylebanese.com.*

Quinoa is a delicately flavored, protein-rich grain. Rinsing removes any residue of saponin, quinoa's natural, bitter protective covering. Find it in natural-foods stores and the natural-foods sections of many supermarkets.

Beans
See also How to Cook Beans, page 191.

Canned beans are convenient but tend to be high in sodium. Give them a good rinse before adding to a recipe to rid them of some of their sodium (up to 35 percent) or opt for low-sodium or no-salt-added varieties. Or, if you have the time, cook your own beans from scratch. Find recipes for cooking beans on the stovetop or in a slow cooker on page 191.

French green lentils are firmer than brown lentils and cook more quickly. They can be found in natural-foods stores and well-stocked supermarkets.

Red lentils are a useful addition to your pantry because they cook in just 10 to 15 minutes. They are excellent in soups, salads and vegetarian stews. You can find them in the natural-foods section of your supermarket or in natural-foods stores.

Nuts & Seeds
To **toast chopped, sliced or slivered nuts**: Heat a small dry skillet over medium-low heat. Add nuts and cook, stirring, until lightly browned and fragrant, 2 to 4 minutes.

Sesame seeds can be purchased already toasted. If you can't find them, toast your own in a small dry skillet over low heat, stirring constantly, until fragrant, about 2 minutes.

Refrigerator & Freezer Items
If you won't be able to use a whole carton of **buttermilk**, you have options. You can substitute 1 cup milk plus 1 tablespoon lemon juice. Or make just the amount of buttermilk you need from powdered buttermilk, which keeps in your refrigerator for several months. Or freeze leftover buttermilk.

To **hard-boil eggs**: Place eggs in a single layer in a saucepan; cover with water. Bring to a simmer over medium-high heat. Reduce heat to low and cook at the barest simmer for 10 minutes. Remove from heat, pour out hot water and cover the eggs with ice-cold water. Let stand until cool enough to handle before peeling.

Greek-style yogurt is made by removing the whey from cultured milk, which gives the yogurt an extra-thick and creamy texture. Look for it with other yogurt in large supermarkets. You can strain regular yogurt to make it thick like Greek-style yogurt. Line a sieve with cheesecloth and set it over a bowl. (*Alternatively, place a large coffee filter in the sieve.*) Spoon in 1 cup nonfat plain yogurt and let it drain in the refrigerator until reduced to ¾ cup, about 2 hours.

Look for balls of whole-wheat **pizza dough**, fresh or frozen, at your supermarket. Or you may be able to buy them from your local pizza place. Choose a brand without hydrogenated oils. If you want to make your own, turn to page 191.

Fruit
To **peel and cut a mango**: Slice both ends off the mango, revealing the long, slender seed inside (*Photo 1, below*). Set the fruit upright on a work surface and remove the skin with a sharp knife (*Photo 2*). With the seed perpendicular to you, slice the fruit from both sides of the seed, yielding two large pieces (*Photo 3*). Turn the seed parallel to you and slice the two smaller pieces of fruit from each side (*Photo 4*). Cut the fruit into the desired shape.

Vegetables
See also vegetable-cooking guides, pages 160 to 165.

To remove **corn** from the cob, stand an uncooked ear of corn on its stem end and slice the kernels off with a sharp, thin-bladed knife.

The dark gills found on the underside of a **portobello mushroom** cap are edible, but can turn a dish an unappealing gray/black color. Gently scrape the gills off with a spoon.

Fresh **winter squash** can be difficult to peel and cut. To soften the skin slightly, pierce squash in several places with a fork. Microwave on High for 45 to 60 seconds, heating it just long enough to slightly steam the skin, to make it easier to peel with a paring knife or vegetable peeler.

Fish & Seafood
For more information about sustainable seafood choices, visit Monterey Bay Aquarium Seafood Watch (seafoodwatch.org) and Blue Ocean Institute (blueocean.org).

The catfish-farming industry has grown in the U.S. and the quality of the fish has improved. Farmers raise **catfish** sustainably in closed pens and feed them a mostly vegetarian diet.

Wild-caught salmon from Alaska is the best choice for the environment, according to Monterey Bay Aquarium's Seafood Watch program. Alaskan salmon is more sustainably fished and has a larger, more stable population. Farmed salmon, including Atlantic, should be avoided, as it endangers the wild salmon population. Wild-caught red salmon, or sockeye, and pink salmon are available in cans too. Unless specified, canned salmon includes the skin and small bones. Although both are edible, we recommend buying boneless, skinless canned salmon (labeled as such) for convenience.

To **skin a salmon fillet**, place on a clean cutting board, skin side down. Starting at the tail end, slip the blade of a long, sharp knife between the fish flesh and the skin, holding the skin down firmly with your other hand. Gently push the blade along at a 30-degree angle, separating the fillet from the skin without cutting through either.

Both **wild-caught and farm-raised shrimp** can damage the surrounding ecosystems when not managed properly. To buy shrimp that have been raised or caught with sound environmental practices, look for fresh or frozen shrimp certified by an independent agency, such as Wild American Shrimp or Marine Stewardship Council. If you can't find certified shrimp, choose wild-caught shrimp from North America—it's more likely to be sustainably caught.

Shrimp is usually sold by the number needed to make one pound. For example, "21-25 count" means there will be 21 to 25 shrimp in a pound. Size names, such as "large" or "extra large," are not standardized.

To **peel & devein shrimp**, grasp the legs and hold onto the tail while you twist off the shell. (Save the shells to make a tasty stock: Simmer, in enough water to cover, for 10 minutes, then strain. Try substituting it for clam juice.) The "vein" running along a shrimp's back (technically the dorsal surface, opposite the legs) under a thin layer of flesh is really its digestive tract. To devein, use a paring knife to make a slit along the length of the shrimp. Under running water, remove the tract with the knife tip.

Meat & Poultry
Andouille sausage is a smoky, mildly spicy pork sausage commonly used in Cajun cooking. Look for it near other smoked sausages in large supermarkets or specialty-food stores.

It's difficult to find an individual **chicken breast** small enough for one portion. Removing the thin strip of meat from the underside of a 5-ounce to 6-ounce breast—the "tender"—removes about 1 ounce of meat and yields a perfect individual portion. Wrap and freeze the tenders and when you have gathered enough, use them in a stir-fry.

To **poach chicken breasts**, place boneless, skinless chicken breasts in a medium skillet or saucepan. Plan on 4 ounces raw chicken for each 1 cup shredded or diced cooked chicken. Add lightly salted water to cover and bring to a boil. Cover, reduce heat and simmer gently until chicken is cooked through and no longer pink in the middle, 10 to 15 minutes.

To trim boneless, skinless **chicken thighs**, use kitchen shears to snip the fat away from the meat.

Grilling Tip
To oil the grill rack, oil a folded paper towel, hold it with tongs and rub it over the rack. Don't use cooking spray on a hot grill.

RECIPE INDEX

Page numbers in italics indicate photographs.

CONTRIBUTORS

Our thanks to these fine food writers whose work was previously published in
EATINGWELL *Magazine.*

BRUCE AIDELLS | Turkish Pasta with Bison Sauce, 47

NANCY BAGGETT | Sweet Potato-Peanut Bisque, 27; Ravioli & Vegetable Soup, 28;
Sweet & Sour Beef-Cabbage Soup, 35; Salmon Chowder, 36; Nut Praline Topping, 181

VANESSA BARRINGTON | Zucchini, Fennel & White Bean Pasta, 55; One-Skillet Bean
& Broccoli Rabe Supper, 102; Bean & Salmon Salad with Anchovy-Arugula Dressing, 147

RUTH COUSINEAU | Chicken Broth, 190

JERRY ANNE DI VECCHIO | Rich Chicken Stew, 94; Slow-Cooked Beans, 191

HEIDI FARNWORTH | Double Peanut Butter-Chocolate Chewies, 171

KATHY FARRELL-KINGSLEY | Frozen Pumpkin Mousse Pie, 176; Grilled Dark
Chocolate Sandwich, 180; Rich Chocolate Sauce, 181

KEN HAEDRICH | Caramelized Bananas, 181

JOYCE HENDLEY | Shrimp Crostini, 155

PATSY JAMIESON | Barley Risotto with Fennel, 78; Grilled Steaks Balsamico, 118;
Hungarian Beef Goulash, 120; Chinese Pork & Vegetable Hot Pot, 123

PERLA MEYERS | Chicken in Garlic-Vinegar Sauce, 93; Pinto Bean & Andouille Sausage
Stew, 124; Calamari, Red Pepper & Lemon Stir-Fry, 151

KITTY MORSE | Okra & Chickpea Tagine, 73

ELLEN ECKER OGDEN | Couscous, Lentil & Arugula Salad with Garlic-Dijon
Vinaigrette, 22

VICTORIA ABBOTT RICCARDI | Amazon Bean Soup with Winter Squash & Greens, 29;
Raspberry-Balsamic Chicken with Shallots, 100

SCOTT ROSENBAUM | Garlic-Roasted Pork, 128

MARIE SIMMONS | Stuffed Tomatoes with Golden Crumb Topping, 112; Grilled Shrimp
with Melon & Pineapple Salsa, 143

BRUCE WEINSTEIN & MARK SCARBROUGH | Grilled Black Bean Nacho Pizza, 44;
Vegetable Fried Rice, 72; Simple Roast Chicken, 85; Beer-Barbecued Chicken, 86;
Chicken & Sweet Potato Stew, 95; Cranberry & Herb Turkey Burgers, 108; Oven Barbecued
Brisket, 119; Middle Eastern Roast Lamb with Tahini Sauce, 135; Cranberry Muesli, 185;
Easy Whole-Wheat Pizza Dough, 191

THANK YOU

Vermont Butcher Block & Board Company for providing beautiful cutting boards for photos.
For more information, visit *vermontbutcherblock.com.*

John Boos & Co., *johnboos.com*

OTHER EATINGWELL BOOKS

AVAILABLE AT EATINGWELL.COM/SHOP

EatingWell 500-Calorie Dinners: Easy, Delicious Recipes & Menus
(The Countryman Press, 2010)
ISBN: 978-0-88150-846-8 (hardcover)

EatingWell in Season: The Farmers' Market Cookbook
(The Countryman Press, 2009)
ISBN: 978-0-88150-856-7 (hardcover)

EatingWell Comfort Foods Made Healthy: The Classic Makeover Cookbook
(The Countryman Press, 2008)
ISBN: 978-0-88150-829-1 (hard

EatingWell for a Heal
Adding Years to Your
(The Countryman Press, 200
ISBN: 978-0-88150-724-9 (ha

The EatingWell Diet:
150+ Delicious, Heal
(The Countryman Press, 200
ISBN: 978-0-88150-722-5 (ha

EatingWell Serves Two
(The Countryman Press, 200
ISBN: 978-0-88150-723-2 (ha

The EatingWell Health
Simple, Everyday Supp
(The Countryman Press, 200
ISBN: 978-0-88150-687-7 (har

The EatingWell Diabe
for Simple, Everyday
(The Countryman Press, 200
ISBN: 978-0-88150-633-4 (ha

The Essential EatingW
(The Countryman Press, 200
ISBN: 978-0-88150-630-3 (har